THE
FINANCIAL
DOMINO
EFFECT

THE

FINANCIAL DOMINO EFFECT

HOW TO PROFIT NOW IN THE VOLATILE GLOBAL ECONOMY

BEN EMONS

New York Chicago San Francisco Lisbon London
Madrid Mexico City Milan New Delhi San Juan
Seoul Singapore Sydney Toronto

1 2 3 4 5 6 7 8 9 0   QFR/QFR   1 8 7 6 5 4 3 2

ISBN: 978-0-07-179958-4
MHID: 0-07-179958-3

e-ISBN: 978-0-07-179959-1
e-MHID: 0-07-179959-1

This publication is designed to provide accurate and authoritative information in regard to the subject matter covered. It is sold with the understanding that neither the author nor the publisher is engaged in rendering legal, accounting, or other professional service. If legal advice or other expert assistance is required, the services of a competent professional person should be sought.
—*From a Declaration of Principles Jointly Adopted by a Committee of the American Bar Association and a Committee of Publishers and Associations*

McGraw-Hill books are available at special quantity discounts to use as premiums and sales promotions, or for use in corporate training programs. To contact a representative, please e-mail us at bulksales@mcgraw-hill.com.

This book is printed on acid-free paper.

*This book is dedicated to my wife Buwon
and my son Derek. For their love and patience.*

Contents

PIMCO Disclaimer

The views contained herein are the author's but not necessarily those of PIMCO. Such opinions are subject to change without notice. This publication has been distributed for educational purposes only and should not be considered as investment advice or a recommendation of any particular security, strategy or investment product. Information contained herein has been obtained from sources believed to be reliable, but is not guaranteed.

This material contains hypothetical illustrations and no part of this material is representative of any PIMCO product or service. Nothing contained herein is intended to constitute accounting, legal, tax, securities, or investment advice, nor an opinion regarding the appropriateness of any investment, nor a solicitation of any type. This publication contains a general discussion of economic theory and the investment marketplace; readers should be aware that all investments carry risk and may lose value. The information contained herein should not be acted upon without obtaining specific accounting, legal, tax, and investment advice from a licensed professional.

Introduction

This book presents a framework on how to analyze and judge the various effects that are intertwined and connected among the sociopolitical environment, the economy, and financial markets. These effects are called *financial domino effects*, analogous to the domino theory first introduced by President Dwight D. Eisenhower in 1954. When thinking of dominoes, one might think of the game that has complex rules with sets that vary in size. In domino games, the players strive to block the movement of the game so that others cannot make a play. In the context of financial markets and economies, however, domino effects are related to cause and effect, wherein events cause a chain reaction of effects as a result of something happening that was unexpected. Domino effects are in fact *unexpected* causality. When events are unexpected, markets tend to overshoot, which can entice policy makers to actions that turn the unexpected events into an economic disaster. Domino effects are also associated with unknown occurrences that can cause what Chicago economist Frank Knight described as "Knightian uncertainty," a reflection of ill-understanding of an event that carries much greater risk than might at first be imagined. Such events are unpredictable, but proper analysis and understanding of domino effects at least may reveal a potential path toward a solution, knowing that uncertainties create tangents. A domino effect has path dependency, whereas market expectations show that the same domino effects could result in many different potential paths.

Many of the recent financial market crises had characteristics of a toppling row of dominoes. In some cases, this happened quickly, whereas the demise of Lehman Brothers saw a rapid unwinding across global markets. Other crises, such as the European debt crisis, still linger, and often new domino effects are revealed as each crisis proceeds. The speed of change is what naturally concerns every investor. Domino effects are aspects of momentum, a change that can become structural. The aftermath of the financial crises saw such structural changes in the economy as well as in markets dealing with the subsequent sovereign debt crises. As crises travel, their journey is covered by effects that accelerate the path toward multiple destinations. This book aims to provide investors with a guide on how to navigate the financial domino effects that seem to be occurring in greater numbers in the financial markets after the era of great moderation.

Part 1

The Fundamentals of the Domino Effects Framework

Chapter 1

Introduction to the Domino Theory and the Framework of Domino Effects

The domino theory explains how a chain reaction occurs as a result of a change in a *structural* relationship. For example, a long-standing political regime in a certain country is successfully overthrown, it gets noticed in other countries, and people in those countries attempt to do the same. Since a small change here causes a similar change elsewhere, it is analogous to a toppling row of dominoes. Such toppling has a certain momentum. It also has a deeper meaning because the change could be permanent. Relationships that stood at the base of a foundation that has been altered through a series of events caused by a chain reaction are known as *domino effects*. The domino theory says that if the energy required to topple each domino is less than the energy transferred on impact, the falling chain of dominoes becomes self-sustaining. And whenever the time between current and successive events narrows, the self-sustaining trend can accelerate.

The domino theory was first mentioned during the Vietnam era; the thought was that if the communists were to succeed in Vietnam, other communists in the region would take note and attempt to top-ple their own political regimes. By early 1954, it was clear to many U.S. policy makers that the French were failing in their attempt to reestablish colonial control in Indochina (Vietnam), which they lost during World War II when the Japanese took control of the area. The Vietnamese nationalists, led by the communist Ho Chi Minh, were on the verge of winning a stunning victory against French forces at the battle of Dien Bien Phu. In just a few weeks, representatives from the world's powers were scheduled to meet in Geneva to discuss a political settlement of the Vietnamese conflict. U.S. officials were concerned that a victory by Ho's forces and an agreement in Geneva might leave a communist regime in control of all or part of Vietnam. In an attempt to rally congressional and public support for increased U.S. aid to the French army, President Dwight D. Eisenhower gave a historic press conference on April 7, 1954. In his famous words, President Eisenhower coined the phrase *domino theory*.

> Finally, you have broader considerations that might follow what you would call the "falling domino" principle. You have a row of dominoes set up, you knock over the first one, and what will happen to the last one is the certainty that it will go over very quickly. So you could have a beginning of a disintegration that would have the most profound influ-ences. But when we come to the possible sequence of events, the loss of Indochina, of Burma, of Thailand, of the Peninsula, and Indonesia following, now you begin to talk about areas that not only multiply the disadvantages that you would suffer through loss of materials, sources of materials, but now you are talking about millions and millions and millions of people. Finally, the geographical position achieved thereby does many things. It turns the so-called island defensive chain of Japan, Formosa, of the Philippines and to the southward; it moves in to threaten Australia and New Zealand.

The domino theory dominated U.S. thinking about Vietnam for the next decade. The Kennedy administration intervened in Vietnam with the purpose of preventing all of Southeast Asia from toppling, where a small country (Laos) was seen as keystone that would accelerate the domino effect through North Vietnam to other neighboring Asian countries. The significant presence of U.S. troops in Vietnam initially may have prevented other communist movements in Malaysia, the Philippines, and Indonesia to succeed, but once the United States pulled its troops out of Vietnam in 1975, a spillover effect occurred into Cambodia, where a bloody civil war between the Khmer Rouge and North Vietnam took place in the late 1970s, and briefly later with a short war between China and Vietnam. A famous quote by MIT Professor Noam Chomsky related to the domino theory: "If people in a poor country see another poor country take control of its economy and succeed, the former will want to emulate the latter." Inspiring to emulate is a cornerstone of the domino theory.

Other elements of the theory relate to causality. In a large domino field, a chain of dominoes can fall, but it also can set off another chain elsewhere in the field. This could have been planned by the designers or driven by totally different factors. Domino effects therefore have elements of *unexpected* causality, a force that leads to a sudden chain reaction. The energy released when the dominoes are toppling can result into a self-sustaining trend because of the upright position of a domino tile. Thus the domino effect can be the result of causality that describes the relationship between an event and a following event, better known as *cause and effect*. The effects can become factors for other effects, influencing events directly or indirectly with or without intervention. The connection between causes and effects is called the *causal nexus*. A chain reaction resembles a sequence of reactions or events in which side effects cause additional responses. A positive or negative feedback loop leads to amplification of the chain of events. In chemistry or physics, when a reaction results in a slow release of energy, it can make way for a greater release of energy that becomes an expanding chain. Frequently such a system collapses or explodes, with release of all the stored energy.

Domino effects are also associated with the concept of a *self-fulfilling prophecy*. This is a prediction that becomes true either directly or indirectly by the very terms of the prophecy itself owing to positive feedback between belief and behavior. Sociologist Robert K. Merton has given the self-fulfilling prophecy the following definition: "When Roxanna falsely believes her marriage will fail, her fears of such failure actually cause the marriage to fail." In other words, the belief that something will change that was at first unimaginable becomes reality. It also has been stated as "think the unthinkable." In Merton's book, *Social Theory and Social Structure*, he describes a bank run as a self-fulfilling prophecy. It is a fictitious bank named Last National Bank, a basic brick-and-mortar bank with liquid assets and investments in business ventures. For unknown reasons, one day a large group of customers shows up all at once. Other customers, seeing so many others standing in line at the bank, get worried, and as rumors spread of problems at the bank, more customers suddenly rush to the nearby ATM or branch to withdraw their money. And so rumors spread further, and more customers show up. By the end of the day, Last National Bank is insolvent. As Merton describes this phenomenon:

> The parable tells us that public definitions of a situation (prophecies or predictions) become an integral part of the situation and thus affect subsequent developments. This is peculiar to human affairs. It is not found in the world of nature, untouched by human hands. Predictions of the return of Halley's comet do not influence its orbit. But the rumored insolvency of Last National Bank did affect the actual outcome. The prophecy of collapse led to its own fulfillment.

Merton's conclusion was that the only way to stop the vicious cycle of self-fulfilling prophecy is by redefining the propositions on which its false assumptions were based originally. However, as the example of the Last National Bank demonstrates, when customers react to other customers and those customers subsequently react, the belief becomes the truth that the prophecy describes, and this is, in fact, very much a domino effect. There are other analogies associated with the self-fulfilling prophecy, such as the *snowball effect*, which a is figurative term for a process that starts from an initial state of small significance and then builds on itself, becoming larger, graver, more serious, and perhaps potentially dangerous or disastrous. Another analogy is a *virtuous* or *vicious cycle*, which is a collection of events that reinforces itself through a feedback loop toward greater instability. Related is the *slippery-slope argument*, which states that a relatively small first step leads to a chain of related events culminating in some significant effect. This is much like an object given a small push over the edge of a slope sliding all the way to the bottom. This is also known as the *camel's nose*, a metaphor for a situation where permitting some small undesirable situation will allow gradual and unavoidable worsening. U.S. Senator Barry Goldwater in 1958 phrased it as follows: "This bill and the foregoing remarks of the majority remind me of an old Arabian proverb: 'If the camel once gets his nose in the tent, his body will soon follow.' If adopted, the legislation will mark the inception of aid, supervision, and ultimately control of education in this country by the federal authorities."

Mark Buchanan's famous book, *Ubiquity*, discusses the theory of chaos, complexity, and "tipping points." In relation to the domino theory, his book details a lab experiment with a pile of sand and how an avalanche has influence on the structure of the pile. The experiment identified certain specific sand grains as having a strong influence, and therefore, when an extraordinary grain touches off an avalanche, a few others keep it going at crucial stages. And since all the grains are identical, it is questionable as to which of them is the real "great grain." Rather, by understanding that the pile is on the edge of some radical change nearly most of the time, one can see that there are always places in the pile where the falling of a single grain can trigger far-reaching and changing effects. These grains are special, however, only because they happened to fall in the right place at the right time. Here is how the sand experiment relates to human behavior. In a critical situation although people have the same abilities only a few would take ordinary action that would have staggering consequences. Some of them may not even be aware of what is happening, but when looking back on history, it may became clear their action propagated significant changes. And although others may have been exceptional, their talent may not be the reason why big events occurred. Nineteenth-century author Leo Tolstoy expresses this in his great work, *War and Peace*, in which he argues that events follow organically from the circumstances of people rather than from the actions of their kings. A famous quote by Tolstoy references to a degree the trigger that may lead to domino-type effects, the trigger being unique to itself:

> When an apple has ripened and falls, why does it fall? Because of its attraction to the earth, because its stalk withers, because it is dried by the sun, because it grows heavier, because the wind shakes it, or because the boy standing below wants to eat it?

And so a grain, an apple, and a person each resembles a unique tile in a domino field. One person, one tile, can make a difference in the direction of the field's course. This relates to causality, wherein a person's actions can cause sudden change. It is also associated with a self-fulfilling prophecy because the person's beliefs make him or her take a certain course of actions. And a domino ties into ubiquity because it may just be a low-ranking person in an organization who achieves just as much significant change as a high-ranking officer. However, a domino also can resemble a company, a government, or a political regime that sets off a chain of events. There are numerous examples of this, such as rogue traders like Nick Leeson causing significant disruption in Asian financial markets, journalists like Bob Woodward and Carl Bernstein uncovering the Watergate scandal that led to the impeachment of President Nixon, the failure of Lehman Brothers caused by the unwillingness of Treasury Secretary Paulson to provide a bailout, and the fall of former Egyptian leader Mubarak, which caused a major political and social shift in the Middle East. The list of examples is long, but what all of them have in common is that a single action caused other effects that had longer-lasting consequences.

Domino effects also exist in relation to path dependency. In economic terms, *path dependency* means that there isn't a unique and predetermined equilibrium. Rather, the equilibrium that is reached at some point depends on the process of the journey followed. Path dependency implies there are different outcomes because there isn't a convergence to a single equilibrium but several equilibria. This is also known as *multiple equilibria*, where markets find two kinds of equilibria—one where demand and supply meet naturally and one where demand and supply do not meet automatically. When certain events become path-dependent, the starting point and subsequent events can influence the outcome—but not without other significant effects. Domino effects, in fact, cause path dependency, as, for example, the Long Term Capital Management (LTCM) and Lehman Brothers crises have shown.

Since domino effects can happen at every level and in multitudes, there is a connection between them. Not surprisingly, as their ubiquity demonstrates, there isn't always one single effect causing more effects, albeit each effect is unique. The uniqueness allows for characterization of domino effects, especially when related to the economy, society, the political spectrum, and financial markets. Their connection is through the transmission of money, power, desire, faith, belief, religion, and so on. As such, this book will focus predominately on domino effects with different time horizons, short and long term, that are influenced by different types of events. Since time and type by themselves can cause accelerated effects, the nature of speed in domino effects plays a great role as well. This brings into the mix the term *momentum*, which is the power residing in a moving object.

The major types of domino effects can be described as follows: There are sociopolitical dominoes that generally entail a change in political regime driven by a splinter movement that responds with discontent. Economic dominoes are related to how a change in consumer and business confidence can change output, growth, and thus unemployment. Financial dominoes refer to how financial markets transmit domino effects. These three major effects are interrelated because one could not happen without the other. If a political figure manages to take over a country and impose capital controls that affect the economy, financial markets will react adversely. Such a chain of events is explained by the domino framework displayed in Figure 1.1.

In principle, a domino effect can start anywhere, for example, an economic recession or even a crisis of some sort can cause political events that may result in military conflict. As the figure shows, the arrows are double-sided between one effect (e.g., economic crisis) and another (e.g., revolution); one can cause the other and return like a boomerang. The figure distinguishes between *types* of domino effects and connects the ultimate effects that lead to corner solutions. Thus, in the case of the Euro debt crisis, economic deterioration as a result of the 2008 global financial crisis and increased government spending owing guarantees to the banking system led to a double-sided crisis, namely, fiscal and financial crises that present two corner solutions—default and inflation. These are in economic terms a potential outcome, in political terms a choice, and in financial terms a solution. The dynamic among outcome, choice, and solution presents interlinkages among events that can drive the three areas together, events that are causal, self-fulfilling, or chaotic in nature. The arrows in the figure highlight this nature, whereas the connections between the different crises, for example, the U.S. housing and European debt crises, constitute an economic, fiscal, and financial crisis. The crises running simultaneously therefore create different outcomes (i.e., war, inflation, and default) in part and are based on how markets and policy makers react.

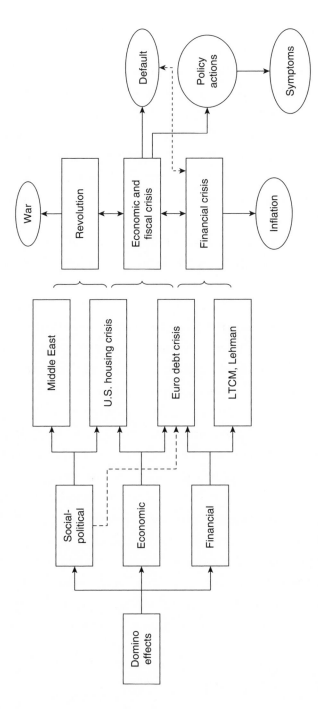

Figure 1.1 Domino framework.

13

There are transmission channels that show how domino effects occur in economies, markets, and society. For investors, it is crucial to identify what type of domino effect exists and what the subsequent sequences and path may be. Underlying this is how the sequence is influenced by how policy makers may respond with actions. What's important is that domino effects are caused by sudden events that lead to a crisis in which the domino effects themselves can accelerate the path of the crisis. This will be a dominant theme of this book, where the different crises and policy reactions will be used to analyze the domino effects and why the crises happened. I present a framework to help investors better understand domino effects and how to recognize them and make appropriate portfolio decisions.

In the following chapters, the framework (as displayed in Figure 1.1) will be discussed step by step. Chapter 2 highlights the three main domino effects with concrete and recent examples. This shows how easily complex domino effects can come into being. Chapter 3 builds on how different transmission channels influence the dissemination and speed of domino effects. Chapter 4 addresses the different kinds of policy responses to domino effects, whereas Chapter 5 goes into the symptoms stemming from those effects. The second part of the book analyzes the elements of the framework by looking closely at the Euro-zone debt crisis in Chapters 6 and 7. The reason why this crisis was chosen and not other crises is that the Euro-zone sovereign crisis is a domino effect of three kinds—social, economic, and financial—that has yet to be played out fully. The consequences of this crisis are far reaching and may have more side effects than commonly understood. The conclusion of this book draws this crisis into a final analysis that attempts to leave the reader with a foundation to navigate different effects in financial markets.

Chapter 2

Three Categories of Domino Effects

Domino effects can be divided into distinct classes. As the basic framework (Figure 1.1) showed, there are three main categories of domino effects:

1. *Sociopolitical.* A political or social movement inspires other movements.
2. *Economic.* A change in confidence and other macro variables leads to a momentum change in the economy.
3. *Financial.* Transmission of socioeconomic, economic, and other information and technical positioning causes rapid changes in markets.

These categories were chosen to distinguish domino effects from one another. As the examples in this chapter will demonstrate, these three main categories have relationships that can lead to a strengthening of correlation between events. In order to better understand how each type of domino effect works, the following sections describe recent examples that fall into one of the three categories.

Sociopolitical Dominoes

Certain events that inspired others were something that happened recently in the Middle East. Protests occurred first in Tunisia and Algeria in late 2010 as a result of a symbolic immolation in response to police corruption. Like a domino effect, protests in Egypt in February 2011 inspired others in Lebanon, Jordan, Yemen, and Syria. The events were driven by the Arab Spring movement, a revolutionary wave of protests across the entire Arab region. The movement involved civil resistance via strikes, marches, rallies, and mass gatherings, and social media played a significant role by allowing communication of common views and raising awareness of state repression and public censorship. Because the demonstrations were met with violence from authorities, they inspired more protests as a result of the media spreading pictures of the violent clashes. This led to a "revolution" in which the political regimes in Tunisia, Egypt, and Libya, after years of being in place, were finally overthrown. As the protests gained further strength, more leaders announced their intentions to step down when their terms expired. In Sudan, Jordan, and Yemen, governments were either sacked or their prime ministers did not seek reelection. Recently, turmoil restarted as the Arab Spring turned to "Arab Winter," wherein political Islam leaped to the fore all across the Arab world. In line with Eisenhower's domino theory, unlike in Southeast Asia, then, the spread of revolution in the Middle East was vast, but it took little to stop it. The Arab Spring/Winter therefore is a sociopolitical domino effect.

In a different fashion, the Occupy Wall Street movement was started on Twitter by the Canadian activist group Adbusters in the summer of 2011. The major slogan used was, "We are the 99 percent," referring to the income disparity between the very wealthy and the rest of the people in the United States. It began as a quiet and peaceful occupation of Wall Street as a protest against corporate America's influence on democracy and the growing income disparity between the rich and the rest of the population, and the repercussions thus far have been largely absent following the 2008 financial crisis. Through the Internet, the activist group Anonymous encouraged its website followers to join the protests centered near Wall Street's iconic statue *Charging Bull.* Once the word spread, more Internet groups in the United States followed the Occupy Wall Street movement. The first protest was held in Zucotti Park on September 17, 2011, which saw follow-on protests across the country in 70 cities. Derivative groups such as Occupy LA and Bank Transfer Day (moving bank accounts to credit unions in order to disadvantage big banks) were further inspired by the media success of Occupy Wall Street. In essence, the movement is a rise of democracy without direct leaders because protests were organized through social media and blogs. Occupy Wall Street has been compared by some to the Tea Party. Others have suggested the movie *V for Vendetta* as a symbolic basis of the movement against corporate greed. In the futuristic movie, the main character, V, after destroying several government buildings, uses media to tell the people of the United Kingdom the truth about its regime and sets a date for action, November 5. V uses a quote, "Remember, remember the 5th of November," to target more government buildings. V ships copies of his mask to all the citizens of London, who then suddenly show up on the night of November 5 to watch V's final act. V went from being seen as a terrorist to being a hero by using the media as his main outlet. In a similar fashion, Occupy Wall Street received a global response because it inspired similar protests in Europe and Asia against the financial industry in the wake of the financial crisis. Because the financial crisis affected many industries and professions, Occupy Wall Street is a reaction to structural unemployment and income disparity. And as that reaction gained success, the popularity of the movement grew across the globe.

Another example is the Euro-zone debt crisis that started in the fall of 2009 when the newly elected Greek government under the leadership of George Papandreou discovered a huge gap in the budget created by the previous government. The realization set in quickly that Greece was basically no longer solvent and needed to be rescued. With a large bailout package of 110 billion euros financed by the European Union (EU) in conjunction with the International Monetary Fund (IMF), Greece has come under life support since April 2010. This life support came with strict conditions and targets set by the EU and the IMF subject to quarterly reviews. From the onset, it became clear that Greece would struggle to meet these conditions unless far-reaching reforms were implemented. The rating agencies such as Standard & Poor's, Fitch, and Moody's repeatedly downgraded Greek government debt, and investors shunned investing in Greek bonds, driving their interest rates into the single digits and further straining the Greek economy. As a result, Greek fiscal targets in 2010 and 2011 were not met because the Greek economy deteriorated quickly. This led to a new bailout package in July 2011 of another 130 billion euros, including involvement of the private sector and privatization of state assets. After more reviews by the Troika (EU, IMF, and the European Central Bank [ECB]) in September and October 2011, the EU and IMF finalized the package, and the Greek parliament signed off on it. That is, the Greek parliament debated it, but the division about the extent of austerity grew so much that the ruling Greek government party, PASOK, and the opposition led by Antonis Samaras collided, which led to a stunning decision by Greek Prime Minister Papandreou to call for a public referendum on October 31, 2011. This threw financial markets into disarray because the referendum had the likely outcome of Greek citizens rejecting the bailout package and Greece potentially facing sovereign default. Equally stunning was the immediate response by German Prime Minister Merkel and French Prime Minister Sarkozy, who openly put the stability of the euro above the Greek crisis and demanded that the Greek referendum be a vote on EU membership.

The call for a referendum led to contagion among European bond markets that spread further, implying that if Greece were able to hold a successful referendum to reject austerity measures, political movements in countries such as Portugal, Ireland, Spain, and even France that are in political and social discontent with austerity would push referenda as well. Public referenda meant to markets a likely rejection of austerity and reforms. This implied that the chance of certain countries becoming insolvent would increase. Again, the element of a domino effect played out as the contagion spread, causing yields on government bonds of European countries to jump one after the other. As the cartoon in Figure 2.1 depicts metaphorically, when Greece started to resist demands by the EU to implement more reforms, its falling statue could have toppled the statues (economies)

Figure 2.1   Euro-zone debt crisis as a potential sociopolitical domino effect.
(*Source:* Kevin KAL Kallaugher, *The Economist*, kaltoons.com.)

of Italy and Spain. Hence the European debt crisis is an example of a sociopolitical domino effect.

Economic Dominoes

Many economic theories describe in some fashion or other a domino type of effect. Keynes' treatise, *The General Theory of Interest and Money*, describes the *multiplier effect*. When the economy goes through a recession and consumer demand and investment fall sharply, government spending needs to be increased. The multiplier effect occurs when government stimuli via higher spending and lower taxes entice business investment, which leads to the hiring of people, who, in turn, spend their income so that aggregate demand in the economy increases. As demand increases, investment increases, and this leads to more hiring and a rise in the gross domestic product (GDP) and so forth. The fact that one event (i.e., government spending) sets in motion other events (i.e., investment and consumer demand) is an example of an economic domino effect. Similar is the *money multiplier*, which measures how much the money supply increases in response to a change in the monetary base. There are several schools of thought, such as the *quantity theory of money*, promulgated by Chicagoan Milton Friedman, advocating modest expansion of the monetary base so as to avoid unintended consequences. Then there is the Cambridge version with the so-called k equation that centers on money demand rather than supply. Both the Chicago and Cambridge schools present multipliers that connect a change in money circulating in the economy with a change in supply and demand. Thus economic multipliers are the amplifiers of economic domino effects, conceptually derived from comparative statics that calculate how much one or more endogenous variables change in the long run given a permanent change in one or more exogenous variables.

Another example of a multiplier is Federal Reserve Chairman Bernanke's concept of a *financial accelerator*. When an economy that is highly financially networked experiences adverse shocks, those shocks can be amplified by financial market turmoil. There is a mutual reinforcement between financial markets and the economy that generally is influenced by a feedback loop that propagates a macroeconomic downturn. The principle of acceleration is the idea that small changes in demand can produce large changes in output.

Thus, when there are meaningful changes in economic and monetary policy, not only do they set off a chain of economic events, but they also work through expectations. A great many theories have attempted explain how such expectations are formed. The most famous is the *theory of rational expectations* by Robert E. Lucas, later advanced by Thomas Sargent. In a nutshell, the core thesis is that people do not make systematic errors when predicting the future, and deviations from perfect foresight are only random. Under adaptive expectations, projections of the future value of an economic variable are based on past values. In other words, the hypothesis of rational expectations assumes that individuals take all available information into account when forming expectations, unlike another theory named *adaptive expectations*, in which people use past information to make predictions of the future. Multipliers and expectations are triggers to momentum in an economy. They complement each other but also contradict each other. As such, multipliers and expectations are economic types of dominoes.

The profession of economics tries to explain imbalances and deviations from some sort of equilibrium. Economic imbalances occur mostly through trade via the current and capital accounts and through expansion of private- and public-sector debt. An economy that has both a current account and a fiscal deficit is said to have *twin deficits*. Before the financial crisis of 2008, such imbalances grew sharply. As can be seen from Figure 2.2, as current-account deficits and surpluses grew larger, trade-weighted exchange rates (a measure of the competitiveness

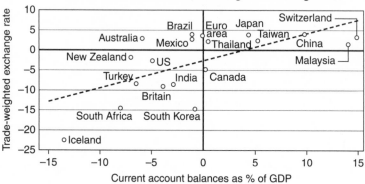

Figure 2.2   Moving Back in Line: Current-accounts deficits versus changes in exchange rates before the 2008 crisis.

(*Sources:* "Economic Focus: The Domino Effect," The Economist, July 3, 2008. This article uses data obtained from BIS.)

of a country) became misaligned. *The Economist* highlighted this in the summer of 2008 with an article titled, "The Domino Effect," that discussed the imbalances as a result of the carry trade. Countries such as New Zealand and Australia have large current account deficits as a percentage of gross domestic product (GDP)—near 7 to 8 percent— and countries such as Japan and Switzerland have equal amounts of surpluses. In the end, it is a zero-sum game because netting all surpluses and deficits should be equal to zero. However, the severity and duration of the imbalance are important and have been cited as two of the underlying factors that ultimately caused the financial crisis. As the figure shows, before the crisis, the imbalances were severe.

The sequence that caused the unwinding of theses imbalances was the U.S. mortgage securitization machine, which proved to be material in funding U.S. consumer spending on low-priced Chinese and other Asian goods during the U.S. housing boom between 2003 and 2006. Based on ultraloose underwriting standards and widespread fraud in mortgage origination, almost unlimited credit was extended to low-income borrowers who were negligent in making their payments from the start. The realization set in by late 2006 that this would become unsustainable because mortgage delinquencies were on the rise at the same time that the U.S. economy was experiencing weakening. In addition, the Federal Reserve's measured-pace tightening of a total of 425 basis points between June 2004 and June 2006 also could have contributed to the explosion in creative mortgage financing that took place, such as pay option, negative amortization, and interest-only adjustable-rate mortgages. It took more than 1½ years for the unwinding of imbalances to begin. The trade imbalance that followed resulted in foreign export nations reinvesting their excess foreign-exchange reserves back into U.S. assets, namely, U.S. Treasury bonds as well as corporate bonds and mortgages. This was the result of a portfolio preference effect driven by a motive centered on foreign creditors maintaining lower-valued currencies to competitively export consumer goods that provided deflation to debtor nations. Such deflation allowed for a measured-pace monetary policy in countries such as the United States in combination with excess reserves reinvestment, producing favorable conditions for asset price inflation. The combination of goods deflation and asset price inflation turned into a positive feedback loop that gave a false sense of hope. The loop drove risk premiums and volatility artificially lower against the backdrop of growing twin deficits. The *twin-deficits hypothesis* says that when an economy is borrowing from foreigners to finance deficits when domestic savings remain the same, sudden currency depreciation or a rise in domestic interest rates can occur. As the twin hypothesis goes, at some point it results in a drastic unwind.

The initial unwind consisted of economic changes in the United States that had domino-style characteristics. Delinquencies started to rise in second liens in 2006, and investors realized that securities made up of packaged loans were perhaps valued less than what their loss and prepayment assumptions implied. When the housing market peaked in late 2005 and housing sales began to slow down, consumer confidence sagged, and the struggling securitization machine provoked a contraction of private credit. The credit contraction was further exacerbated by distrust among banks to lend to each other. Banks also were reluctant to borrow from the Fed because of fear of stigma. This combination let to a credit contraction that sparked a greater economic slowdown, and as that process continued, consumer confidence fell, as reflected in stock market losses and declining economic output, leading to a further drop in new home sales, which fed back via falling asset prices into reduction of consumer spending and thus a rise in unemployment. The fall in confidence, output, asset prices, and employment is a sequence not unlike a domino effect: Each individual economic variable is driven by unique factors, yet they set each other in motion.

Financial Dominoes

Domino effects occur that are separate from what the political spectrum and the economy witnessed in financial markets. Either they are a reaction to policy developments, or they can be technical in nature. The distinction between technical and fundamental reasons for domino effects often has been referred to as *financial* or *technical contagion*. During financial crises such as those in Thailand in 1997, Russia in 1998, and the United States in 2008, technical contagion was caused, for example, by positioning in derivatives markets. When the hedge fund LTCM fell in 1998, the fundamental reason for its collapse was a political regime in Russia that no longer honored its debt obligations and defaulted. The excessive volatility that followed snowballed across global markets. This was exacerbated by less well understood externalities of the large derivatives positions LTCM had taken on with numerous counterparties. It resulted in a technical domino effect, whereas LTCM derivative complexities led to an unwinding of other positions as a result of margin calls. The Federal Reserve Bank of New

York orchestrated the first major financial bailout of LTCM through a consortium of banks. The LTCM failure was a precursor to the global financial crisis that followed a decade later with even greater intensity. Thus, because a political regime led to a technical change in markets, the result was an impact on the real economy. This influenced thinking within the Fed that asset price volatility had to be factored into monetary policy decision making. Up to the present, the technical and fundamental domino effect of the LTCM crisis is still having an effect on the economy, as, for example, the recent debt crisis in the Euro-zone shows.

The Middle East turmoil in 2011 also had an effect on financial markets because the change in a long-standing political regime in Egypt sparked a surge in oil prices that provoked preemptive tightening by global central banks such as the ECB, as well as the Bank of Brazil. Combined with uncertainty from Europe's debt crisis, preemptive tightening by the ECB caused a financial crisis in the European banking sector. This is a financial domino effect, an effect that moves quickly through markets that are ultraefficient in processing new information. Federal Reserve Chairman Bernanke gave the domino effect a different name when he called the Fed's large-scale asset-purchase program QE2, short for "quantitative easing part 2," a virtuous circle. When the Fed lowers long-term interest rates, the effect is higher stock prices, with a stronger economy emerging. In addition, profit expectations rise, which, in turn, drives stock prices up further, and thus growth accelerates. However, with emerging-market countries already experiencing higher growth and inflation, the growth impact of QE2 drove inflation expectations up and enticed economic tightening by more emerging-market central banks. Four dominoes—the Middle Eastern Arab Spring, the European debt crisis, the U.S. economy and debt ceiling debate, and emerging-market inflation—are affecting global markets each in their own way, and the spillover among them can manifest as a change in a specific price. When the Egyptian political turmoil

escalated, it caused a sharp rise in the price of oil that increased inflation expectations not just in emerging markets but also in developed
markets. The result was early tightening by the ECB. Former ECB
President Jean Claude Trichet justified this tightening by saying that a
central bank cannot control or set the price of commodities, only the
price of liquidity. Early in January 2011, markets anticipated that the
ECB would make an adjustment via higher interest rates as commodity
prices rose further. This anticipation, however, once more highlights
how expectations can be validated by forcing a central bank to react to
a price—the price of oil—that the central bank cannot control.

There are three "prices," namely, the price of oil, the price of
European government bonds, and the price of AAA-rated sovereign
bonds, and each can act as a catalyst for all three major domino effects.
There could be more, such as the price of gold, equity prices, volatility,
and others. This is one aspect of domino effects: A sharp change in the
price of oil may cause a sharp rise in other prices, such as the prices of
gold, Swiss francs, and U.S. Treasuries. The economic slowdown on
the back of higher gas prices, combined with the uncertainty created
by the developments in the Middle East and Europe, can entice the
Federal Reserve to attempt more stimulus while structural deleveraging of private-sector debt remains ongoing. The higher energy prices,
on the other hand, push the ECB to tighten and cause further deterioration in the liquidity of European sovereign bonds, and the higher
prices (or rates), in turn, force European politicians to put in place
more austerity measures. Those austerity measures weaken the economy, which weakens the domestic banks that hold government bonds,
and the banks, in turn, are forced to deleverage by regulatory means
as a result of the perceived weakness of sovereign bonds. The uncertainty creates further strain on the global economy because European
banks withdraw credit from the tradable sector and so forth. This sets
in motion a vicious and virtuous circle that leads to wedges in markets,
as demonstrated in Figure 2.3.

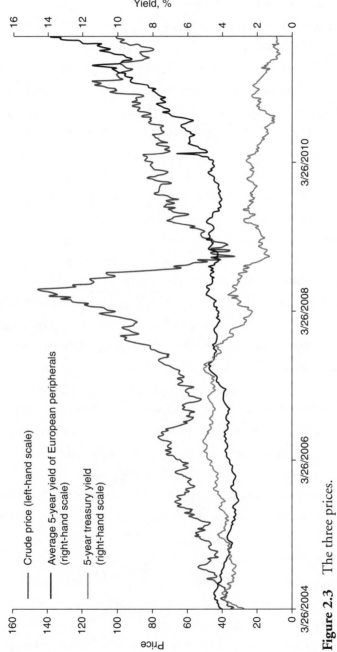

Figure 2.3 The three prices.

(*Source:* Bloomberg.)

27

A financial domino effect also has an element of *flight to quality*. This can be driven by two types of mechanisms—either an amplification or a balance sheet mechanism. The amplification mechanism occurs when risk aversion becomes excessive because unusual events have unknown outcomes. When the news of the tsunami broke in March 2011, the precarious situation surrounding Japan's Fukushima Dai-Ichi nuclear reactors could have had catastrophic financial consequences. The market reaction was a big drop in Treasury yields, interest and currency volatility spiked, and global stock markets sold off sharply as the drastic economic effects of the nuclear disaster were discounted. This shows that an amplification type of flight to quality can turn into a balance sheet type, and vice versa, creating a sense of Knightian uncertainty, a reflection of poor understanding of a tail risk event such as a total nuclear breakdown in Japan or the potential for serial sovereign bond defaults in the Euro zone.

In his Semiannual Monetary Policy Report to the Congress on March 1, 2011, Federal Reserve Chairman Bernanke indicated that if the debt ceiling weren't extended, the United States would face the risk of default and thereby cause a serious change of heart in its creditors. Bernanke judged that confidence could be eroded if the political capacity were insufficient and brought forward the risk of perpetual gridlock. If the result of such gridlock is a failure to extend the debt ceiling, this might create a new kind of financial crisis because banks that hold Treasury bonds rely on receiving timely interest and principal payments and thus could be unable to make other payments. The loss of confidence in the deepest, most liquid market would affect other assets, as reflected in the demand for higher Treasury interest rates by creditors, which would increase the uncertainty of whether the U.S. government could obtain funding. The fiscal problems could multiply because rising interest costs are part of the deficit, requiring deeper spending cuts and tax increases. Bernanke was right in hindsight because the impasse between President Obama and Republican

House Speaker Boehner grew deeper during the summer of 2011. As a result, Standard & Poor's (S&P) lowered the U.S. credit rating from AAA to AA+ on August 6, 2011, and kept the outlook negative by citing the following:

> We lowered our long-term rating on the U.S. because we believe that the prolonged controversy over raising the statutory debt ceiling and the related fiscal policy debate indicate that further near-term progress containing the growth in public spending, especially on entitlements, or on reaching an agreement on raising revenues is less likely than we previously assumed and will remain a contentious and fitful process.

On December 5, 2011, S&P also put all remaining AAA-rated European countries on a negative rating watch, stating that there were ". . . continuing disagreements among European policy makers on how to tackle the immediate market confidence crisis and, longer term, how to ensure greater economic, financial, and fiscal convergence among Euro-zone members."

Fitch followed S&P on December 16, 2011, by revising the outlook for France and making Italy and Spain more negative with the following statement: "Following the EU Summit on 9–10 December, Fitch has concluded that a 'comprehensive solution' to the Euro-zone crisis is technically and politically beyond reach."

These statements introduced a new kind of domino effect—a rating agency questioning the ability of a once-perceived "safe" government to be creditworthy. Once the United States was downgraded, the whole spectrum of remaining AAA-rated countries came into play. Since Japan is no longer rated AAA, the trend in U.S. and German credit default swaps (CDSs)—contracts between two parties that the seller will compensate the buyer in the event of default relative to Japan—became one of *convergence*. In part, the convergence reflects expectations of a ratings downgrade for Germany sometime in the future. An additional fact is that the U.S. downgrade changed the notion of the risk-free rate. Theoretically, the *risk-free rate* is the boundary of an investment with no loss. The assumption as to why a rate of return is risk-free is that there is little or no possibility of a government default. And in a flat currency–based system, the government, through its central bank, has the ability to print unlimited amounts of currency to pay debts. In essence, the risk-free rate reflects the government's temptation to print money when debt payments become very difficult or impaired. A large debt-to-GDP ratio with the prospect of a rating downgrade could be a positive factor for nominal bond yields. The reason for this is that such a downgrade affects contractual rates in the economy and thus broader financial conditions. It can lead to a flight to safety to government bonds that can have a sequence and momentum. A sequence occurs because German government bonds benefit from the prospect of a U.S. downgrade occurring well before a German downgrade. And momentum is seen because the U.S. debt impasse leads to a reduction in growth and inflation expectations in Japan as U.S. rates fall in relation to those of Japan.

Because printing money to pay debts simply devalues the risk-free rate by debasing the currency, a relevant question is, How long can the risk-free rate be "guaranteed"? Thus there is a differentiation of the risk-free rate within global government bond markets. Those markets, such as the United States and the United Kingdom, where a central bank anchors short-term rates keep the yield curves steep. This can increase the volatility premium in the long end of the yield curve as expectations of inflation and growth are pushed out further in time. Markets such as those of Italy and Spain, where the government is constrained as a result of having inherited large debt in an economic downturn—in other words, markets with limited fiscal capacity—may see the short end of their yield curve bearing a higher risk premium because low growth increases the risk of government insolvency. Aside from the absolute direction of bond yields, rating downgrades affect the shape of the yield curve, and that can push banks, companies, and consumers toward an adverse change in financial conditions.

AAA-rated sovereign CDS differences went through several stages of convergence. Because this was linked to the European debt crisis, when the crisis intensified, so did the convergence. Since Japan was the one major sovereign without an AAA rating (Japan is rated AA–/Aa3), CDS markets implied that contingent liabilities taken on by Euro-zone countries to bail out other countries and the extended fiscal stimulus of the United States, described as "kicking the can down the road," eventually would result in all remaining AAA-rated sovereigns likely losing that status in the next year or two. However, like a domino effect, as contingent liabilities grow, as well as the temptation to kick the can down the road, rating agencies will react and could lower ratings. Those ratings are hardwired into the bond benchmark universe and investor guidelines. Thus, as the AAA spectrum shrinks, so does the available risk-free rates that function as a discount rate in equity and corporate bond valuations. The unsafe feature of sovereign bonds also causes a migration to other emerging-market sovereigns that are lower rated but perceived to be safer owing nonexistent contingent liabilities and government guarantees for their private sectors. And as a result, there also has been a rating migration as capital flight has lowered emerging-market bond yields, which with a proactive monetary policy and limited expansionary fiscal policy have stabilized and improved their sovereign ratings.

On January 13, 2012, S&P downgraded France and Austria to AA+ and kept the Netherlands and Finland at AAA but with a negative outlook, whereas Germany also remained AAA but with an outlook upgraded to stable. The immediate inclination was that Germany became the sole stable AAA government, and as a result, investors responded, and further flights to quality into German government bonds occurred. Flight to quality was once more driven by market participants seeking safety by increasing demand for government-backed assets and reducing demand for privately backed assets. The AAA downgrade of France produced a similar effect, whereas German government

bonds were perceived to be ultrasafe, while the effect also was technical as a result of AAA benchmark portfolios proactively reconfigur-
ing their allocation. Another implication of the downgrades was the
two-tier effect, whereby in downgrading France and Austria but not
Germany and the Netherlands, S&P created another wedge between
the AAAs (Germany versus the Netherlands and Finland) and the
former AAAs (Germany versus France, Austria, the Netherlands, and
Finland).

Lessons

What sociopolitical, economic, and financial dominoes all have in
common is that they are driven by a reaction that follows from other
reactions. Such reactions, however, can be a lagging response owing
to the fact that initially a change isn't noticed. That effect also has
been analyzed along the concept of a J-curve. This is explained as the
relationship between a country's stability and its social and political
openness. The idea is that countries start off closed and stable and
end up open and stable. The meaning of J-curve is also related to
imbalances—a currency devaluation worsening a trade deficit at first
as the prices of goods lag followed by an improving deficit. A J-curve
also can be placed in the context of complacency, a self-satisfaction
accompanied by an unawareness of danger. Such complacency shows
up at times in financial markets. When risk premiums are narrow,
equity prices are high, volatility is low, and real rates are negative,
the combination provides a "cocktail" of complacency that proves
to have a bitter aftertaste. Like a J-curve, complacency can swing
toward paranoia, and a domino effect of unwinding risk positions
may follow. Figure 2.4 attempts to depict the idea of a J-curve of
complacency, a large wedge between negative real rates, risk assets
such as gold, distressed assets such as Euro-zone peripheral bonds,
and low volatility and risk premiums. Such a wedge proved to be a

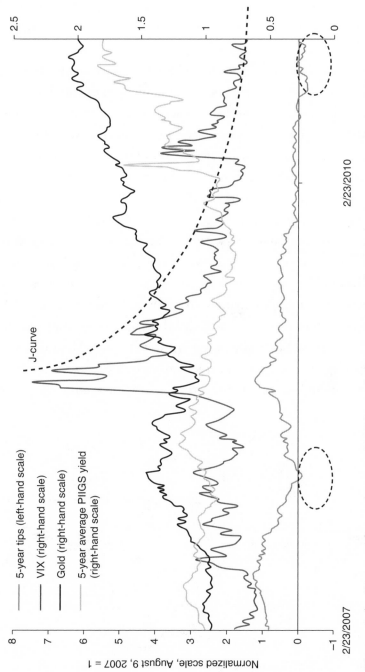

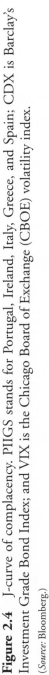

Figure 2.4 J-curve of complacency. PIIGS stands for Portugal, Ireland, Italy, Greece, and Spain; CDX is Barclay's Investment Grade Bond Index; and VIX is the Chicago Board of Exchange (CBOE) volatility index.

(*Source:* Bloomberg.)

33

precursor in 2007 of what was yet to come in terms of a financial crisis. Amid the current sovereign crisis, this figure shows that such a wedge appeared.

Thus, to arrive again at the framework introduced in Chapter 1, the combination of the sociopolitical, economic, and financial domino effects produced *multiple crises*. The crises may result in multiple outcomes driven by the three prices, each in connection with the others and each unique in its own way. The domino framework becomes more complex as more effects are layered on top of each other. The recent string of cases shows how a socioeconomic movement caused a spike in oil prices that had an effect on U.S. trade deficits and several peripheral European economies as well as a breach of inflation targets. In reaction to this, policy makers of several central banks tightened interest rates and language, which, in turn, had an effect on the interest rates on government bonds, namely, those of Euro-zone peripherals. As those interest rates rose and the peripheral economies were affected by the higher crude oil price, the rating agencies responded with downgrades and negative outlooks. This lead to responses from officials on the pan-European level calling for further reforms and austerity to win

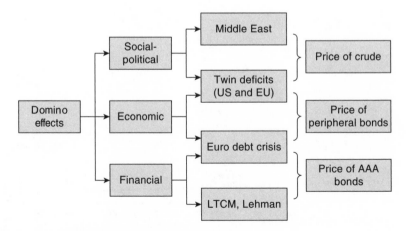

Figure 2.5   Domino framework revisited.

back the confidence of the markets, whereas such measures pressured the already battered peripheral economies in addition to the adverse effect of higher crude prices. The key point here is that domino effects have a strong direct and indirect multidimensional linkage to portfolio decisions. As Figure 2.5 shows, the outcomes also multiply from inflation, default, and flight to quality, downgrades, and policy tightening at the same time. These outcomes are linked through transmission, and how these linkages work will be discussed in detail in Chapter 3.

Chapter 3

Channels of Contagion, Transmission, and Spillovers

Transmission is the process by which the various channels of monetary and fiscal policy are transmitted through financial markets into the real economy. The literature on this topic is vast. From an academic perspective it is important to understand how domino effects can be caused by several methods of transmission. Transmission and domino effects are closely related because they both result from an amplitude or multiplier. The difference is that transmission may be a policy-induced reaction to domino effects. That said, it is also true that unintended domino effects can occur whenever transmission is under way. The basics of transmission lie in identifying channels and how they function in markets. The main transmission channel is the nominal interest rate, whereas a change in nominal rates affects economy-wide contract rates as well as the cost of capital for companies. There are other channels, such as wealth, credit, exchange rates, and what's called the *monetarist channel*. This monetarist channel is how nonconventional monetary policy such as quantitative easing is transmitted. Central banks each have their own views on how monetary transmission works. In part,

37

this is driven by their mandate, which can be single and explicit (e.g., for the European Central Bank, price stability, and for the Bank of England, an inflation target), implicit (e.g., for the Bank of Japan, a midpoint for inflation), dual (e.g., for the Federal Reserve, inflation and employment), and quadruple (e.g., for the Bank of China, inflation, growth, and exchange rates). Figure 3.1 presents an example of monetary transmission taken from the European Central Bank. An immediate take from the diagram is that it looks like a domino field. Moreover, the effects from changes in official rates through the expectations channel has a profound impact on short-term (i.e., less than two years) interest rates, credit, asset prices, and eventually the price level in the economy. This is a financial domino effect through the monetarist channel.

There is also a concept of *sovereign transmission.* This occurs when deterioration in sovereign creditworthiness affects the funding of banks

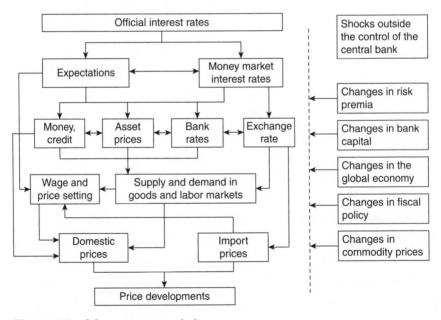

Figure 3.1   Monetary transmission.
(*Source:* European Central Bank.)

directly through an earnings impact from sovereign holdings or indirectly owing to sovereign rating downgrades resulting in bank downgrades, reductions in collateral value in the form of government bonds held for wholesale funding, and reduced benefits from implicit or explicit government guarantees. There is a *confidence channel* of businesses and the private sector where policy makers use such signals as changes in rules, regulations, or policy that markets, businesses, and people anticipate. Such anticipation leads to action and perhaps even a permanent change in spending or investing behavior. The main objective of transmission is to restore the functioning of a market, mechanism, or distorted economic relationship. Often there is a liquidity shortage that can affect sectors of the economy, individuals, and governments. Transmission is connected to domino effects via a type of virtual loop or vicious or virtual circle. For example, when a bond issuer, private or sovereign, experiences a price decline in its bonds, this could give rise to questions about the underlying financial condition of the issuer, which, in turn, could create a crisis of confidence without a fundamental underlying basis. When a change in confidence spills over, it can cause a rapid adjustment in assets prices and thus might instigate a reaction by market participants as well as central banks. These events are interlinked as market participants act quickly and the central bank responds, which can provoke another reaction by market participants. Such a reaction is called a *feedback loop* that can enhance or buffer changes in a system. A *positive* feedback loop enhances or amplifies changes; it tends to move a system away from its equilibrium state and make it more unstable. A *negative* feedback loop tends to dampen or buffer changes; it tends to hold a system to some equilibrium state and make it more stable. The situation becomes more complex when microfactors enter in, such as a bank run. As Robert K. Merton described in his self-fulfilling prophecy theory, such a run happens when rumors take hold that make the public believe that a financial institution is in trouble. A colleague at Pacific Investment Management Company

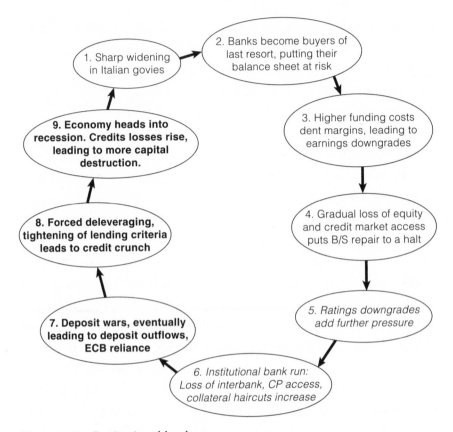

Figure 3.2 Institutional bank run.
(*Source:* PIMCO.)

(PIMCO), Philippe Bodereau, who heads the financial credit research department, has identified a feedback loop that shows how bank runs happen. The example here again involves sovereign transmission, where a fall in government bond prices initially drags the banks into buying bonds that subsequently are confronted with a solvency crisis that has a severe impact on the banks' liquidity. A solvency crisis then turns into a liquidity crisis. Figure 3.2 shows how this feedback loop becomes repetitive, where funding costs, rating downgrades, and deposit wars lead to a self-enforced deleveraging of the banks' balance sheets that feeds directly into the economy.

A shortage of liquidity also can affect governments. Government liabilities are largely future tax receipts. When there is belief that a government is solvent, the market rewards the government by allowing it to borrow at a risk-free rate. When there is doubt, investors demand a higher rate that could reach a level where the solvency of a government is in serious question. And the higher the level of government debt (in combination with high nominal interest rates) rises above a country's nominal gross domestic product (GDP), the shorter the distance becomes between solvency and default. The markets then also will make no further distinction between interest rates associated with solvency and interest rates associated with default. When domestic banks are the main investors in the sovereign bond market, their balance sheets are very exposed to government bonds. When domestic liquidity gets scarce, deposits are harder to roll over, and banks have to pay punitive interest rates on their bank debt. This happens even for banks that are "healthy" and sound when the sovereign crisis spills over into the banking system. Greece and Portugal, as well as Spain and Italy, have been confronted by such spillover risk caused by a change in perception of their sovereign solvency.

This leads into another situation in which domino effects are created, namely, through *spillover effects*. These are externalities of economic activity or processes that affect those who are not directly involved in such economic activity. Moreover, here channels play a crucial role. To see what happens in such a situation, one need only look at the holdings of foreign sovereign debt by domestic banks. When a sovereign debt rating is downgraded, it conceivably could affect the profitability of banks in other countries if those banks are holding some of that sovereign debt. In the case of Europe, for example, many European banks at times hold substantial amounts of sovereign debt in both their trading books and banking books, and news of a sovereign rating downgrade may "spill over" across borders. Specifically, when the banks in one country hold claims on banks in other countries, this creates a situation of double exposure. This cross-border holding feature was at the core of the European debt crisis and was a product of the financial market convergence process that occurred in Europe during the late 1990s into the 2000s.

Crises can happen in contemporaneous ways. There can be a common cause that leads to similar effects in different countries. There also can be a crisis in one country that triggers a crisis elsewhere for unexplained macroeconomic reasons but generally is due to market sentiment shifts or changes in interpretation of information that is given. A domino effect that happens because the macroeconomic fundamentals in one country owing to currency devaluation changes the relative price competitiveness between countries is a linkage spillover. Direct trade linkages between the countries serve as channels where spillover effects can be very adverse. In such a context, they can be called a *chain of causation*, where an adjustment in the trade balance of a large economy lowers production and growth in an export-dependent nation. A global collapse of trade in a synchronized manner after the financial crisis results in a sequential bank trade credit freeze. A chain of causal economic events is an economic domino.

Spillover effects are closely associated with *channels of contagion*. These channels function mainly through asset markets, where information about economic, political, and social instability is transmitted instantly. A country may pursue a policy of exchange-rate stabilization that could lead foreign-exchange dealers to revise their expectations about other countries. An attack on one currency and the issuing government's response to the pressure thus may provide new information relating to expectations of how other governments will respond if placed in a similar position. In such a crisis, there is a spillover effect where an attack on one country's currency causes attacks elsewhere. An example of this is the "tequila effect" in Mexico in 1994, where trade links functioned as a transmission channel for currency contagion that spread quickly across Latin America, followed later by Asia.

There is also an element of skepticism at work in which attempts to stabilize a currency are called into question. Such uncertainty actually leads to further currency pressure and subsequent resumption of attacks, where one government's response to the pressure may provide new information relevant to expectations of how other governments will respond if placed in a similar position. Trade links suggest that a currency crisis can spread contagiously among countries that trade disproportionately with one another. Economic and political commonalities suggest that instability could infect countries in broadly similar economic and political positions.

For example, say that a country with a high unemployment rate succumbs to a speculative currency attack and abandons its currency peg out of reluctance to raise interest rates because that would adversely affect its current accounts through the capital account. When the pound sterling was attacked in September 1992 and subsequently devalued, it is said to have damaged the competitiveness of Ireland, for which the United Kingdom is the single most important export market, and to have provoked the subsequent attack on the Irish punt at the start of 1993. Finland's devaluation in August 1992 was widely regarded as having had negative repercussions for Sweden, not so much because of direct trade between the two countries but because their exporters competed in the same third markets. Attacks on Spain's currency in 1992–1993 and the depreciation of the peseta are said to have damaged the international competitiveness of Portugal, which relies heavily on the Spanish export market, and to have provoked an attack on the escudo despite the virtual absence of imbalances in Portugal's domestic fundamentals.

There are other definitions of contagion. *Currency contagion* has a dual meaning: technical contagion when markets adjust through positioning and fundamental contagion when entire economic systems or countries are affected. An example of technical contagion is the Japanese yen carry trade. This trade stems from the basics in foreign-exchange trading. A foreign currency that has a higher interest rate over a domestic currency is said to exhibit *carry*, the term for the interest-rate differential an investor can earn over the life of the currency position. For example, if an investor were to purchase Brazilian reals versus the U.S. dollar when Brazilian interest rates are currently at 9 percent and U.S. interest rates are 0.25 percent, the investor would earn 8.75 percent in carry. That occurs, of course, only when the interest-rate differential remains unchanged over the term of currency contract. A currency carry trade is also engaged when an investor can borrow in a currency with a very low interest rate and use the funds to buy higher-yielding assets elsewhere. Since 1997, when the Bank of Japan's main policy rate fell below 1 percent, the carry trade became a staple, with the most popular strategy to exploit the gap between U.S. and Japanese government bond yields. As described briefly in Chapter 1, hedge fund Long-Term Capital Management (LTCM) popularized the yen carry trade by using significant leverage (100 times in some cases) to borrow yen at 1 percent or below and purchase higher-yielding instruments. In addition, a carry trade has a double payoff profile: the interest-rate difference and currency appreciation. The yen carry-trade proxy is to borrow in yen at low rates and reinvest the proceeds in 10-year U.S. Treasury bonds or 10-year German bunds. On average, an investor could earn about 1 to 1.5 percent in carry on top of the yield earned on the bond position. The carry trade saw violent unwinds during the LTCM crisis in 1998, during the financial crisis of 2008, and recently during the Euro debt crisis when Asian investors fled Italian and other bonds.

A more recent example of a large carry trade occurred in early 2009 when the global economy began to recover from the collapse after the financial crisis. At that time, companies were undergoing synchronized inventory restocking, there were equally synchronized fiscal and monetary stimuli, and the April 2009 G-20 meeting in London called for concerted action to counter fragile demand and confidence, as well as to promote growth, fight against protectionism, and provide sufficient funds to prevent cross-border contagion. The G-20 members committed themselves to maintaining the supply of credit by providing more liquidity and recapitalizing the banking system, as well as rapidly implementing stimulus plans. The central banks pledged to maintain low-rates policies for as long as necessary. The combination of these actions, as well as the beginning of recovery in economies, ignited a trend toward risk across markets. As this happened, confidence in economies returned, and because emerging-market economies didn't suffer that much from the fallout of the financial crisis, growth, especially in emerging markets, returned quickly back above trend. The backdrop to all this was the carry trade in the weakening U.S. dollar—described by Nouriel Roubini in the *Financial Times* of November 1, 2009, as "the mother of all carry trades." The fact that the U.S. dollar turned into a funding currency like the Japanese yen constituted the precrisis. Because the Federal Reserve pledged to keep interest rates low for some time, the borrowing rate implied as a result of the dollar currency was in fact negative, which occurs when one central bank keeps rates unchanged while the central bank of the foreign currency intends to raise its interest rate. Nouriel Roubini estimated that the implied borrowing rate based on the U.S. dollar was in fact 10 to 20 percent negative on an annualized basis. This opportunity allowed risk-appetite investors to borrow supercheap dollar funds to reinvest in higher-yielding assets elsewhere. The embedded contagion was that the risk of all assets was masked by quantitative easing policies that dampened volatility when, in fact, the correlation between asset prices was close to one as they rose simultaneously. Once quantitative easing effects fade, asset prices deflate, which indeed they did, so when quantitative easing 1 (QE1) and QE2 ended, the domino effect was that all asset prices fell, which then spilled over to confidence in the real economy. This explains why several central banks such as the Fed, the Bank of England, European Central Bank (ECB), and even the Bank of Japan restarted their easing cycles in late 2011 in response to asset price volatility and financial distress.

In a different context, contagion also simultaneously has been called a *monsoon effect*. This is seen when there is a seismic shift in economic conditions in large industrial countries that triggers a crisis in less developed countries. The contagion effect works through the channel of currency borrowing, the level of outstanding government debt, and the financial state of the domestic banking system. During the 1980s, several emerging-market debt crises were caused to a degree by the sharp rise in interest rates in the United States as a result of Paul Volcker's monetary policy. During the mid-1990s, the appreciation of the dollar versus the Japanese yen was seen as an important factor that contributed in the erosion of several Southeast Asian countries' export positions. More recently, in 2011, rising crude prices as a result of turmoil in the Middle East, combined with easy Federal Reserve policy that weakened the dollar, led to preemptive tightening by the ECB to avoid higher energy costs being passed on to workers via wages, the so-called second round effect. The tightening of 0.5 percent in the ECB policy rate during the first half 2011 affected liquidity conditions in European sovereign bond markets, which as a result saw a further increase in government bond yields. A monsoon is an indirect domino effect, something caused by other sets of factors.

The phenomenon of contagion was a major theme in the European debt crisis. Thus far the crisis has displayed characteristics of currency contagion, where through spillover effects one country's bond market undergoes pressure that causes more pressure in neighboring markets. The element of skepticism appeared frequently when European policy makers repeatedly attempted to stabilize the bond markets, but their efforts were called into question by markets. Such market behavior compounded uncertainty that actually led to further pressure. And it presented a test: One government's crisis response to its bond market may provide new information relevant to expectations of how other governments may respond. Thus, in this context, contagion has a dual cause—trade links that spread a currency crisis contagiously among countries with high intratrade (i.e., trade between countries in close proximity). Economic and political commonalties spread the infection to countries with broadly similar economic and political positions.

The channels of contagion were very familiar in Europe. Intratrade, current-account imbalances, and banking systems with large cross-border sovereign holdings all functioned as channels to spread sovereign bond risk around Europe. Contagion had a side effect on other sovereign markets with large deficits, such as the United States and the United Kingdom, which benefited from a flight to quality, accentuated by their central banks actively purchasing government bonds. But contagion also found encouragement through the political channel. In Europe, it became a virtuous circle: Contagion provoked a reaction by policy makers to enforce austerity, markets reacted with skepticism, and this led to even more austerity. While this was happening, the European debt crisis saw a jumper effect—from summit to summit and event to event—each time spreads widened further, as shown in Figure 3.3.

In an empirical study published by the Dutch Central Bank (DNB), Mark Mink and Jakob de Haan attempted to quantify the contagion effect during the Greek sovereign debt crisis from April 2010 to November 2010. The researchers used a sample of 48 banks across the Euro zone that held Greek bonds and had other peripheral bond exposures as well. The main finding of the study was that news disseminated about Greece itself didn't result into excessive bond price returns, whereas the news about a bailout for Greece did. The empirical test spanned 20 days, sampling extreme returns on Greek sovereign bonds. During that time, the average bank experienced a return equal to 3.26 percent on its stock when the news was positive and –1.62 percent when the news was negative. The research further showed that news about the economic situation in Greece didn't have a material

Figure 3.3   Contagion effect on European sovereign spreads.
(*Source:* Bloomberg.)

effect on the market capitalization of sample banks. Additionally, any news related to the possibility of a bailout of Greece did affect the stock prices of the sample banks. As measured empirically by the study, a 1 percent change in Greek government bond prices induced by news about a bailout on average resulted in a 0.124 percent change in the sample banks' market value. The DNB research presented two findings. The first one implied that market participants did not alter their expectations about the losses that banks would suffer in the case of a Greek default in response to news about the economic situation in Greece. The other finding showed that the prospect of a Greek bailout was a stabilizing factor for bank stock prices. Thus, when Greek bond prices rose owing to positive news of a bailout, bank stock prices were positively correlated with bonds. Markets therefore viewed positively the willingness of governments to backstop banks from losses on their sovereign exposures by bailing out a country like Greece that in case of default may have had a snowball effect. The determination of the DNB paper was that a plausible explanation for the impact of news about Greece on other countries was a learning effect or, in other words, a "wake-up call." This effect addresses the concept of a crisis that initially is restricted to only one country may reveal new information about how such a crisis is handled. In the case of poor management, it could prompt investors to reevaluate where else such vulnerability may be evident. The risk aversion that is brought forward out this kind of investor behavior can be a catalyst to quickly spread the crisis across borders. The DNB research concludes that the ability of one country to reduce deficits and debt in a credible manner is tested by markets and rating agencies and becomes an informative event on how likely other countries will be capable of reducing debt levels. These learning effects showed up in the DNB research as an explanation of why other countries' bond markets experienced wild swings in returns, especially after the news about Greece's situation was digested.

The return swings in European bond markets were not always caused by speculative attacks but rather by liquidations by long-term investors such as pension funds, insurance companies, passive index funds, and banks. These liquidations brought *collateral contagion* to the surface. Collateral contagion is related to stigma: A bank holds lots of sovereign bonds that are viewed as toxic, and its ability to maintain funding therefore disappears quickly. The bank starts to liquidate its sovereign holdings, and the resulting rise in yields provokes more liquidations. On the other hand, collateral contagion in which secured lending, based on sound assets, has replaced unsecured lending is seen as a shortage of available collateral. This shortage was caused by a few factors: repurchase agreement (repo) market shutdown owing to higher failure penalties, reduction in pledged collateral owing to counterparty risk restrictions, increased collateral haircuts, higher margins on derivatives, and greater safekeeping at central banks. This is a direct result of banks having to shrink their balance sheets for regulatory reasons (e.g., Basel III) and because of contagion. During the financial crisis of 2008, the contagion went through securitized mortgage loans that banks held in vast amounts on their books and were later transferred to government bonds. In a recent study, the International Monetary Fund (IMF) estimated an overall reduction in collateral to the tune of $5 trillion from the peak in 2007.

Since collateral is scarce, along comes creativity, which causes further scarcity as a source for contagion. There are *liquidity swaps*, where banks on the periphery swap illiquid assets such as real estate loans for more liquid ones such as German government bonds from other banks. Peripheral banks then turn around and pledge the liquid assets at the ECB, thereby further reducing the availability of liquid collateral. There is *collateral transformation* for central clearing of derivatives, where custodian banks turn (transform) customers' less liquid assets such as corporate bonds into central counterparty clearing-eligible securities. These inventions have clear limits because they rely on intermediate private funding markets. They present another channel of contagion because during times of distress, transformed or swapped collateral will require greater haircuts.

Whenever transmission, spillovers, and contagion occurs, they happen because a *tipping point* has been reached. The tipping point is the critical point in an evolving situation that leads to a new and irreversible development. The term is said to have originated in the field of epidemiology, when an infectious disease reaches a point beyond any local ability to control it from spreading more widely. Malcolm Gladwell, in his book, *The Tipping Point*, describes the idea as follows: "Whenever critical mass is achieved, a certain moment was a boiling point, a threshold." A tipping point is also described as a turning point or, metaphorically, a point of no return.

Financial markets experience such moments now and then. The Lehman Brothers collapse now has become one of the most famous ones. The early morning hours of Monday, September 15, 2008, served as moments of panic and confusion, as well as an opportunity to liquidate and to start shopping for distressed assets that had value. In other words, the Lehman Brothers event was, in short, chaos, an apparent lack of order in a system that nevertheless obeys particular laws or rules. Along with chaos theory, the financial system in 2008, no matter how complex it was, relied on an underlying order that stated that very simple or smaller systems and events can cause very complex behaviors or events. This is known as *sensitive dependence on initial conditions*—the slightest difference in initial conditions that are beyond human ability to measure can make predictions about past or future outcomes impossible. Famously described in 1963 by Edward Lorenz as the *butterfly effect*, where a single flap of a single butterfly's wings would be enough to change the course of all future weather systems on earth. Lorenz refined the butterfly effect, stating, "Predictability: Does the flap of a butterfly's wings in Brazil set off a tornado in Texas?" The example of such a small system as a butterfly being responsible for creating such a large and distant system as a tornado in Texas illustrates the impossibility of making predictions for complex systems. Despite the fact that these situations are determined by underlying conditions, precisely what those conditions are can never be sufficiently articulated to allow long-range predictions.

This is what precisely happened during the demise of Lehman Brothers. The firm played an integral role in derivatives markets, and the scope of the intertwined aspect of the counterparties Lehman Brothers was facing was unknown to market participants and policy makers. When former Treasury Secretary Hank Paulson, then New York Federal Reserve Bank President Geithner, and Fed Chairman Bernanke met separately during the September 13–14, 2008, weekend of Lehman Brothers' buyout negotiations, Paulson reportedly used the dogma of former Treasury Secretary Mellon in the 1930s: "Liquidate labor, liquidate stocks, liquidate the farmers, liquidate real estate, to purge the rottenness out of the system." Paulson stood fast that after the bailout of Bear Stearns in March 2008, the U.S. taxpayer should not be on the hook for more bailouts. From an Austrian economist's point of view, this was the right thing to do. Because of the complexity and leverage of the financial system, Paulson's rebuttal caused an unwind that began rapidly through a chain reaction: a run on money-market funds after it became known that one of the largest money-market funds, Reserve Primary Funds, revealed that it owned significant amounts Lehman Brothers debt. The Reserve Primary Fund broke the buck on its daily net asset value mark that was a pretense: Money-market funds maintain an artificial price of $1 per share, promising investors at all times a dollar in, a dollar out, plus interest, on demand. Reserve Primary held $785 million in commercial paper issued by Lehman Brothers Holdings, Inc., and the company failed, and the fund no longer had enough assets to ensure that customers could retrieve all their money. The fund tried to meet redemptions by selling its investments into a panicking market. This led to a contagion effect that spilled over to other money-market funds, with the result that in the span of two weeks, $400 billion was pulled out, and the flow of short-term credit from the funds to companies froze. Another chain was London-based hedge funds that relied on Lehman Brothers for day-to-day financing. They found themselves unable to do business because their accounts with Lehman Brothers' U.K. subsidiary were frozen. Because of Lehman Brothers' large global operations, similar dislocations played out around the world, and a paralysis of fear and distrust contaminated the entire financial system. It became known as a *credit tsunami* that affected global trade in particular, whereby letters of credit were frozen. Of the $13.6 trillion of goods traded worldwide, 90 percent rely on letters of credit or related forms of financing and guarantees such as trade credit insurance, according to the Geneva-based World Trade Organization. Letters of credit are centuries-old instruments that allow far-flung partners to complete large transactions. Suppliers of oil, coal, grain, and consumer products from Chicago to Mumbai suffered large losses on sales as the credit crisis spread beyond financial institutions, culminating with banks refusing financing or increasing the fees for buyers. Coupled with the overall decline in global demand that started in the summer of 2008, the credit squeeze severely affected international trade. Technical contagion from derivative unwinds led through a sequence of events to fundamental contagion. Or rephrased, a financial domino effect (i.e., the financial crisis) turned into an economic domino effect (i.e., trade collapse) that eventually had sociopolitical consequences. The aftermath of the financial crisis proved dire in terms of the U.S. unemployment rate, which stubbornly stuck at around 8 percent. This caused political shifts in the House and Senate, multiple fiscal stimuli, and, moreover, a loss of competitiveness as skill mismatches within the U.S. economy rose to all-time highs.

There is another aspect to the 2008 financial crisis, and that is that its underlying root cause was credit derivatives. In 2000, David Li wrote the infamous paper, "On Default Correlation: A Copula Function Approach." The *copula formula* attempts to predict the likelihood of various events occurring when those events depend to some extent on one another. Conceptually, Li modeled probabilities of default by drawing inspiration from "broken hearts": People who experience the death of a beloved spouse tend to die faster. This is otherwise described as a *Markov chain*—a series of statistical events whose outcomes depend on one another. But Li acknowledged in 2005 after the General Motors mini–financial crisis that his model had flaws. For one, the model assumptions rely on a snapshot of credit-spread curves rather than on a real-time version that takes into account the movements of those curves. The result is that the actual prices in the market often differ from what the model indicates they should be. The assumed events in Li's model were clustered around an average, like a normal distribution. The model was capable of capturing binary outcomes such as life or death, but in mortgages or economics, such outcomes can be more random. Moreover, unlike a binary outcome, the correlation between such variables as mortgage delinquencies and consumer spending increased, in that defaults among consumers also increased the default risk within banks holding vast numbers of consumer loans. A default correlation that the likelihood of default for the underlying pool resembles that for all the companies, consumers, or other entities is high when credit risks look identical. The correlation is lower if the credit risks are more uneven. Standard & Poor's published empirical research on default correlations and found that as an economy increasingly becomes more finance- and credit–based, the correlation between defaults and bankruptcies in the financial sector and other sectors in the economy increases sharply over time. When this correlation changes between year 1 and year 5, the correlation between sectors also increases.

The relevance of this research is in the context of a *balance sheet mechanism*. This is a transmission channel that reflects the financial institutionalization of financial markets and economies. It explains a feedback loop between asset prices and balance sheets and how this relationship can change investors' liquidity preferences. When balance sheets become dependent on asset price behavior, a negative asset price shock suddenly tightens investors' balance sheet capacity, which forces them to liquidate assets. The preference shift that goes from more liquid and less risky assets can further lower asset prices and thereby deteriorate balance sheets that serve as an amplifier to the initial shock. The default correlations are an additional factor that comes into play; that is, through the balance sheet mechanism, market technical factors become procyclic and influence economic fundamentals. When this happens, policy responses occur in several ways, a topic of discussion in Chapter 4.

Chapter 4

Policy Responses

Whenever a crisis occurs, monetary and fiscal policy makers react. Their response is motivated by objectives such as an inflation target, political reelection, or even an emergency. Since the 1990s, when the financial crisis intensified in nature, the policy response has become more intense as well. This is a direct result of the fact that economies are becoming increasingly asset-financed. As the deregulation of banking globally allowed for more entrepreneurship in the creation of credit, since the 1970s, many economies have transformed into capitalists economies. Hyman Minsky describes this well in his *financial instability hypothesis*: "the characterization of the economy as a capitalist economy with expensive capital assets and a complex, sophisticated financial system." The consequence is that economies work more in "real time" as equity and bond markets reflect dynamically the economy's daily generated net worth. Such real-time exposure influences spending and investment decisions as well as expectations. These are fueled by a net present value (NPV) effect, the fact that an economy's finance rate can instantly adjust companies' and individuals' financial existence or people's ability to borrow and spend. The NPV of net worth, however, is based on expectations of future earnings extrapolated to a current value. These expectations depend greatly on what future interest rates will be. Hyman Minsky worded this as follows:

> As a result of the process by which investment is financed, the control over items in the capital stock by producing units is financed by liabilities—these are commitments to pay money at dates specified or as conditions arise. For each economic unit, the liabilities on its balance sheet determine a time series of prior payment commitments, even as the assets generate a time series of conjectured cash receipts.

In other words, by comparing the present value of future expectations with today's net worth, there is an incentive to borrow and spend earnings that still need to be made. Spending tomorrow's future today is a key feature of a capitalistic economy.

The loop discussed in Chapter 3 is shown once more in Figure 4.1, where the NPV of assets is central. Any of the modern and major developed economies has this fundamental base, and this is why since

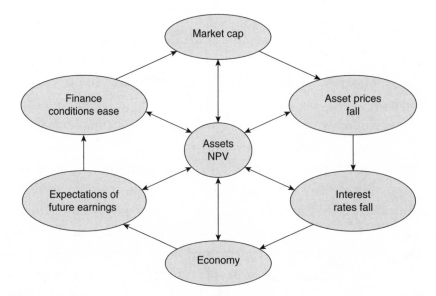

Figure 4.1   NPV effect of the economic cycle.

the 1990s the Federal Reserve (as well as other central banks) has cut interest rates aggressively to restart the NPV effect of assets. This would entice borrowing behavior owing to a positive wealth effect, whereby future living standards are brought forward to current living standards even though, in reality, those living standards actually don't improve. The reason is that leverage is what drives such artificial wealth creation, especially when leverage is applied through a lightly regulated financial system such as the *shadow banking system* that funds itself through uninsured and unsecured debt markets. When credit problems arise and debt levels are too high relative to income because of (inflated) assumptions about asset values and perpetual income levels, central banks lower their rates to ease debt-service costs that stand in direct relation to debt-to-income ratios. Hyman Minsky identified three types of units when speaking of the debt-to-income relation: hedge, speculative, and Ponzi. The Ponzi unit, according to Minsky, is based on "cash flows from operations [that] are not sufficient to fulfill either the repayment of principle or the interest due on outstanding debts." Such units have to either sell assets or borrow more to meet obligations, so Minsky judged that "a unit that Ponzi finances lowers the margin of safety that it offers the holders of its debts." It is these types of units that can accelerate the asset NPV cycle. The highly speculative or Ponzi-like nature of an asset economy can have a negative feedback loop enter the NPV cycle that becomes self-fulfilling through a series of domino effects. Hyman Minsky's theory in essence links financial domino effects to the business cycle he saw as capitalist because government interventions and regulations keep the NPV system within boundaries. The NPV effect, however, can diminish when asset values and income are reduced to such a low level that debt reduction becomes a downward spiral. This spiral can be self-defeating unless a grand-scale official intervention is conducted by a central bank using monetization or governments using fiscal spending.

Central Bank Intervention

Prior to the 2008 financial crisis, global monetary policy was traditional and conventional. Its function as "lender of last resort" had a dual mandate:

1. The short-term interest rate was the main policy tool to maintain price stability—the benchmark policy rate.
2. The stability of the banking system was supported and safeguarded by liquidity provisions and supervision through use of the effective policy rate.

Before the 2008 crisis, global central banks could be divided into three distinct groups: (1) those employing implicit/explicit inflation targeting, (2) those employing growth targeting, and (3) those employing exchange-rate targeting. Global central banks before the crisis formed a "triangle" as part of the monetary agreement that has been described as *Bretton Woods II*, a new international system involving an interdependency between states with generally high savings in Asia lending and exporting to Western states with generally high spending. The system was supported by the monetary agreement between central banks with different objectives but the same traditional tools.

Central banks predominately in Asia and Latin America were targeting their exchange rates artificially low as part of a growth strategy that focused intensely on expansion of trade. Through the trade channel, lower-priced goods from Asia provided deflationary pressure to major developed economies with their inflation-targeting central banks such as the Bank of England, the European Central Bank (ECB), and the Federal Reserve. Dooley, Landau, and Garber argued that the Bretton Woods II system, composed of (semi)fixed and heavily managed exchange rates, was fundamentally stable, and with the required intervention, the currencies of Asian countries would not appreciate and therefore would provided the bulk of the financing of then (2006) $600 billion U.S. current-account deficit (today it stands at $450 billion based on Bloomberg figures). As a result, reserve accumulation of dollars by China, Russia, Japan, and other central banks stands at cumulative $10 trillion in foreign-exchange reserves that are reinvested into U.S. Treasuries, U.K. Treasuries (gilts), and German government bonds (bunds). As a result of this reinvestment policy, government bond yields in major developed markets remained lower than what they otherwise might have been, helped in part by the deflationary trend coming from Asian goods prices owing to exchange-rate targeting by Asian central banks. Thus the combination of relatively low interest rates in major economies and stable inflation expectations, inflation-targeting central banks ran policy-tightening cycles that in fact became lengthier after 2000. When interest rates were slashed during 2007–2008, the cycle shifted to the *zero bound*, a profound and dramatic change. The zero bound is a constraint that limits policy makers using traditional tools, the benchmark, and an effective policy rate. Because the zero bound has been in place since 2008 for major central banks, this has moved those central banks toward deploying creative and different types of tools.

The post–financial crisis global economy was weakened substantially and in the process revealed a severely impaired credit transmission apparatus as a result of unwinding of the shadow banking system. Traditional policy changed to the unconventional, a switch to measures such as *quantitative easing* (QE) and *credit easing and competitive quantitative easing* (CQE). These policies in general have a twofold purpose:

1. Improvement of credit conditions within the banking system and capital to enhance lending and borrowing
2. Increasing the money supply to lower (long-term) interest rates, thereby stimulating investment and consumer demand

Quantitative easing (QE), as in nonsterilized purchases of (mostly government) debt by a central bank, has its roots in the 1930s. In 1937,

John Hicks, in response to Keynes's theory, argued that the supply and demand for bonds had a direct relationship to the supply and demand for money. As the demand for money falls owing to interest rates rising, people prefer to buy interest-bearing bonds and hence save more than they spend. In the case of an economy that experiences output expansion, the demand for money rises, and people would liquidate their bond holdings to increase spending. Hicks developed this idea within the *IS-LM framework*, which is the relationship between output (Y) and interest rates (r) expressed by the investment savings (IS) curve, which is downward sloping (as interest rates rise and output falls and vice versa), and the money supply (LM) curve, which is upward sloping (as interest rates fall and demand for money falls [supply rises] and vice versa).

Within this framework, when fiscal policy expands, the IS curve shifts to the right, and thus output is stimulated through the Keynesian multiplier effect. However, Hicks's point was that the Keynesian multiplier could be hindered if the demand for money stayed low as interest rates remained relatively high. Monetary policy could support the Keynesian multiplier by increasing the monetary supply (which would shift the LM curve downward) and thus lower (long-term) interest rates and increase the demand for money and stimulate spending. The downward shift in the LM curve would go through open-market operations, where the central bank purchases government bonds from the banks and the public. When the LM curve shifts to the left and the IS curve shifts to the right, a new equilibrium is found in which output expands. This is shown graphically in Figure 4.2.

Another definition of QE is the expansion of bank deposits held at a central bank. By increasing such deposits with money creation and offering low or even negative rates on them, the cash flood banks experience can lead to a spillover into assets and thus into the economy as a whole. QE during 2009–2010, however, saw deposit expansion in reverse: The central bank purchased assets from the regular banks, which, in turn, saw their reserves increase and put those on deposit

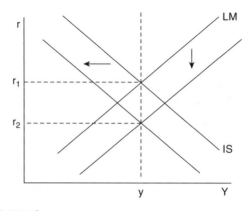

Figure 4.2   IS-LM diagram.
(*Source:* N. Gregory Mankiw, *Macroeconomics,* New York: Worth Publishers, 1994.)

back at the central bank. The most evident has been the ECB's deposit facility, which saw an explosion in 2011 as the ECB expanded its non-conventional measures with loans to banks (LTROs). Such measures are actually more *credit easing*—expansion of reserves that assist in the refinancing of bank-issued debt. Federal Reserve Chairman Bernanke explained in a speech early 2009 the benefits of credit easing because of its specific focus on a mix of loans and securities affecting credit conditions for households and businesses. QE, with its sole focus on bank reserves, was in Bernanke's view extending central bank liabilities via government bond purchases. The asset mix in QE had a more "incidental" composition feature, namely, portfolio exposure in short- and long-dated government bonds. Credit easing liquefies distressed assets, so a *flow effect* occurs as primary issuance restarts. QE changes the creditor status of government liabilities from the private sector to the central bank, resulting in a *stock effect.* Programs such as the Fed's Term Asset-Backed Securities Loan Facility (TALF), the ECB's Covered Purchase Program 1.0 and 2.0, and the Bank of Japan's Term Lending are examples of credit easing. The effectiveness of these programs occurs through reduction of liquidity risk in distressed assets by secured central bank funding. Key to liquefying a frozen relationship between creditor and debtor is that the asset is viewed as solvent. Thus credit easing is a form of "nonstandard" discount window lending by providing government liquidity using private assets as collateral. Through the central bank's *special-purpose vehicle* that buys the assets by secured term lending and adding a nonrecourse and guarantee feature, liquidity risk embedded in spreads is reduced dramatically.

Since the Bank of England announced QE in early February 2009, other central banks followed soon after in an almost coordinated fashion. The reasons to do so have varied—the Federal Reserve mainly supporting the housing market, the Bank of Japan expanded its existing Rin Ban operation, the Swiss Central Bank attempting to stem CHF exchange-rate appreciation, and the ECB supporting the covered bond market to restore medium-term funding for European banks. Other central banks, such as the Bank of Canada, the Riksbank, and the Norges Bank (although a fund was established to purchase assets), are opting to implement QE. All these actions fall under the name of monetary easing, but since the action was carried out by each central bank for its domestic financial market, it also can be called *competitive quantitative easing*. This also was seen in the 1930s, when the United Kingdom abandoned the gold standard, allowing a devaluation of the pound, and several other countries followed with devaluations. These devaluations were known as *competitive devaluations* because they sought to boost trade. In 2009, major developed economies experienced severe recessions for similar reasons—a credit contraction—so the central banks acted in their own interest. Central banks followed each other in a competitive way, absent a coordinated response. Thus global QE also became known as *competitive QE*.

QE's Effects

The intention of QE was different from that of credit easing—it was a rebalancing effect. As a result of the banks signaling QE, investor anticipation drove portfolio allocations into U.S. Treasuries. When

Treasury yields became very negative in real terms, this pushed investors into equities, corporate bonds, and other assets that had positive
real rates. The premise of this strategy was that portfolio assets are
imperfect substitutes. By drastically changing the yield of so-called
risk-free assets, a domino effect occurred in other assets, which is
the *portfolio rebalancing effect*. The true intention of QE therefore
was to generate a self-feeding mechanism of expectations building on
expectations in a way similar to that of the money multiplier. During
QE, the Federal Reserve succeeded with this strategy because the
portfolio balance had a knock-on effect on its favorite gauge of inflation expectations, the 5-year/5-year forward breakeven derived from
Treasury inflation-indexed securities. This is a market-based measure
in which investors assess what inflation will be in five years. The
positive correlation between the change in the Fed's balance sheet
and forward breakeven inflation shows a direct connection with the
rise in asset prices, as shown in Figure 4.3. Each time the Fed balance
sheet expands from QE, returns on equities rise and inflation expectations move upward.

The Federal Reserve and the Bank of England have published
extensive research on the effects of QE and other nonconventional
measures. The New York Federal Reserve Bank published a paper
by Brian Sack in 2010 titled, "Large-Scale Asset Purchases by the
Federal Reserve: Did They Work?" This paper highlights specifically the announcement effect of QE on U.S. Treasury bonds (UST)
and mortgage-backed securities (MBS) rates and modification of the
purchase-amount language at subsequent meetings. Longer-term interest rates declined by up to 150 basis points around key large-scale asset
purchase (LSAP) announcements. LSAP announcements reduced the
10-year term premium by between 30 and 100 basis points. Study
shows that few of the observed declines in longer-term yields appear to
reflect declining expectations of future short-term interest rates associated with Federal Open Market Committee (FOMC) communica-
tions about the likely future path of the federal funds rate.

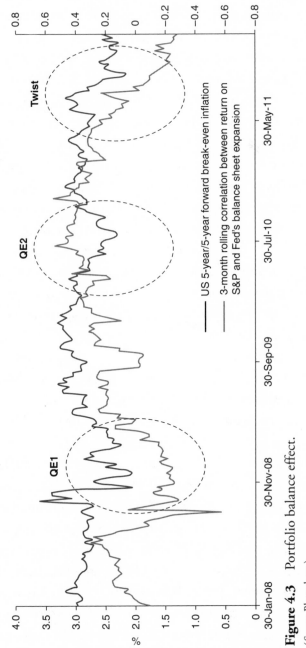

Figure 4.3 Portfolio balance effect.

(*Source:* Bloomberg.)

Another paper, by Christopher Neely, "The Large-Scale Asset Purchases Had Large International Effects" (2010), extends Sack's analysis looking at the announcement effect of U.S. LSAP on international rates and currencies. LSAP buy announcements significantly reduced long-term foreign bond yields and the spot value of the dollar. On the days QE was announced, foreign bond yields declined by an average of 45 basis points, including Japan. Excluding Japan, the average across Australia, Canada, Germany, and the United Kingdom was close to 60 basis points. LSAP announcement weakened the U.S. dollar versus major currencies on the announcement day by 2 to 3 percent on average. Throughout the first purchase program period (March 2009–March 2010), the U.S. dollar lost 20 to 40 percent versus the Australian dollar and the Norwegian and Swedish kronas but just 6 to 10 percent versus the euro, pound sterling, Japanese yen, and Swiss franc.

A different paper by Neely, "The Effects of Large-Scale Asset Purchases on TIPS Inflation Expectations" (2010), looks at the announcement effect of QE on Treasury inflation-protected securities (TIPS) inflation expectations. In a two-day window of the announcement of QE, inflation expectations appear to react modestly to LSAP announcements (between 7 and 18 basis points). Inflation expectations appear to rise after the announcements, however, which implies that LSAPs may have limited power to raise TIPS-implied inflation expectations.

More specifically, a paper by Stefania D'Amico and Thomas King, "Flow and Stock Effects of Large-Scale Treasury Purchases" (2010), goes into intraday changes in yields when the purchases occurred (this is different from the first Neely paper, where the author examines intraday changes in yields as a result of announcing QE). Each purchase operation, on average, caused a decline in yields in the sector purchased by 3.5 basis points on the days when these purchases occurred: the *flow effect* of the program. In addition, the program as a whole resulted in a persistent downward shift in the yield curve by as much as 50 basis points, the *stock effect*, with the largest impact in the 10- to 15-year sector. Specifically, the average purchase operation temporarily reduced yields by about 3.5 basis points, and the program as a whole shifted the yield curve down by up to 50 basis points.

A study for the San Francisco Federal Reserve Bank by Reuven Glic and Sylvain Leduc, "Central Bank Announcements of Asset Purchases and the Impact on Global Financial and Commodity Markets" (2011), shows that commodity prices tended to fall, on average, on announcement days, especially during QE's first phase (2009–2010). The research shows that indices for energy prices and precious metals tended to decline significantly during the round of announcements, and the results suggest that "market participants viewed LSAP announcements by the Federal Reserve as signaling lower future economic growth in the United States, which jointly lowered long-term interest rates, the value of the dollar, and commodity prices on the days that policy news was released." Glic and Leduc judged that "positive surprises" associated with an easier monetary stance tended to "lead to declining long-term interest rates and *falling* commodity prices." In contrast, negative monetary surprises led to "significant increases in long-term interest rates but to flat or weak increases in commodity prices."

There also was a study by Hess Chung and Jean-Philippe Laforte titled, "Estimating the Macroeconomic Effects of the Fed's Asset Purchases." In this simulated study, the QE program would raise the level of U.S. real gross domestic product (GDP) by approximately 3 percent in 2012. The boost to real output affects labor market conditions "noticeably better than they would have . . . without large-scale asset purchases, benefits that are predicted to grow further over time." The researchers also concluded that by 2012, the completion of QE would have an incremental positive contribution to employment, estimated as creation of around 3 million jobs. This increased hiring would lower the unemployment rate by 1½ percentage points compared with what it would have been absent the Fed's asset purchases. The San Francisco Federal Reserve Bank research concluded further that QE is an "equivalent amount of support to real economic activity through conventional monetary policy" that "would have required cutting the federal funds rate [by] approximately 3 percentage points." Early in 2011, Fed Chairman Bernanke laid out in his testimony before Congress the same rule of thumb: $600 billion worth of QE purchases is the equivalent of a 75 basis point rate cut from the fed funds rate. Bernanke based this rule of thumb on QE in 2009, where it was shown that $150 billion to $200 billion of Treasury purchases were worth a rate cut of about 25 basis points. This was measured by the effect of the purchases on Treasuries and mortgages, whose rates fell as they normally would have in the past when the fed funds rate was lowered by 25 basis points.

So QE worked in the United States as an interest-rate cut, where the NPV effect on assets was evident based on percentage change in the domestic equity markets, narrowing of corporate bond spreads, and falls in mortgage, consumer, and Treasury rates. As the San Francisco Federal Reserve Bank study simulated, the actual change in employment indeed so far has been on track by a mere 155 thousand average jobs per month created, and the unemployment rate indeed had fallen from 9.7 percent in November 2010 to 8.5 percent by the start of 2012. The same is the case for core inflation, which rose from 0.8 to 2.2 percent by late 2011, and this demonstrates that the asset NPV effect still worked by slashing other interest rates, even if official rates were at the zero bound. QE is a "virtuous circle" in which the Fed lowers long-term rates, and the effect is higher stock prices with a stronger economy emerging and rising profit expectations, which, in turn, drive stocks up further, and thus growth can accelerate. Above all, QE is a financial and economic type of domino effect.

The Bank of England conducted its own two studies. The first was titled, "The Financial Market Impact of Quantitative Easing," by Michael Joyce, Ana Lasaosa, Ibrahim Stevens, and Matthew Tong. This study concludes, like the Federal Reserve research, that QE in the United Kingdom may have depressed gilt yields by about 100 basis points, and the largest part of QE's impact came through a portfolio rebalancing channel. The paper also concludes: "The wider impact on other asset prices was more difficult to disentangle from other influences: The initial impact was muted, but the overall effects were potentially much larger, though subject to considerable uncertainty." Another paper by the same authors, "The United Kingdom's Quantitative Easing Policy: Design, Operation and Impact," indicates that an important factor is the impact of QE, but even more important is how that policy was transmitted. Figure 4.4 is a diagram taken from that paper, which shows the relevant transmission channels.

QE also has effects that can multiply. Like domino effects, they create momentum and set off a chain reaction in other asset markets and thus potentially broadening the economy. The figure therefore is a relevant diagram showing how QE transmission is a sequence that can start more sequences. The signaling effect is what has been cited as powerful because it allows the policy maker to have the market do half the work. This consists of more follow-on effects that have a repeating manner—signal, anticipation, announcement, implementation, and expiry.

This is the *QE sequence*. By signaling the policy intent, it moves markets into the targeted asset with the same policy, whereby anticipation turns into realization by other investors who can't afford to stay much behind. By the time the policy is announced officially, it has created sufficient arguments in the eyes of investors for them to rotate out of risk-free government bonds into riskier assets. When investors do so, the central bank starts its purchases at improved economic levels, and by being the consistent demand factor, it replaces a spike in interest rates with a gradual daily rise. This adjustment in rates reflects a perception of the economic cycle that turns normally rather than one

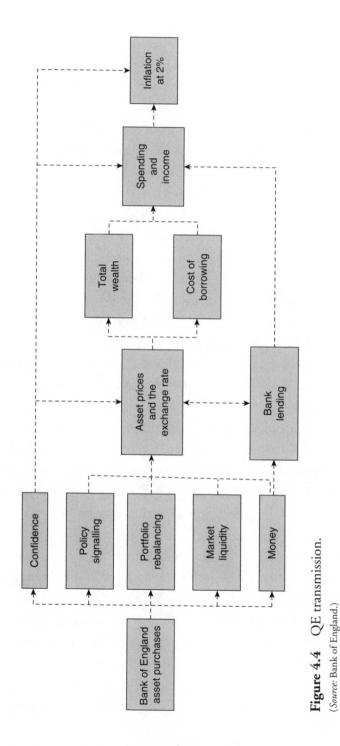

Figure 4.4 QE transmission.
(*Source*: Bank of England.)

that experiences expectations of a sudden turn in inflation. Figure 4.5 illustrates the repetitive nature of QE1 and QE2 and shows how signal, anticipate, announce, implement, and end series evolved during 2009 and 2011.

This figure also shows how the sequence of QE effects took place as of November 2008 when the Federal Reserve first signaled the possibility of using QE, followed by the Bank of England in early 2009. The sequence had a repetitive character, whereby the policy maker signals his or her intentions, and combined with deteriorating macro fundamentals, that intention warrants such a signal, market expectations anticipate policy action, followed by an announcement and subsequent implementation and end effect. Federal Reserve and Bank of England research efforts have proven empirically that this is true, as described in the preceding paragraph, but Figure 4.5 shows how these different effects altered forward bond yields, a market expression of expectations. The change in expectations also changed investment behavior, such as in going from being invested in cash and T-bills to reinvesting those into riskier assets such as high-yield commodities and equities. As mentioned previously, this is called the *portfolio balance effect of QE*.

QE not only changed risk behavior through portfolio balancing, but it also created a liquidity competition among banks for the wealth effect from government bonds in the early stages of the recovery in 2009. This liquidity competition was driven by the central bank, which essentially was motivated to create a comparative credit advantage to jump-start its domestic transmission. When the central bank supplies the liquidity by printing money, capital-constrained domestic banks use the yield curve to extrapolate the carry by buying government bonds. However, when the central bank influences secondary bond prices and thereby the composition of all outstanding bonds, QE brings along a second-order effect—demand elasticity for newly issued government bonds. From microeconomic theory, this is perhaps best known as *cross-price elasticity of demand*—the demand of a good

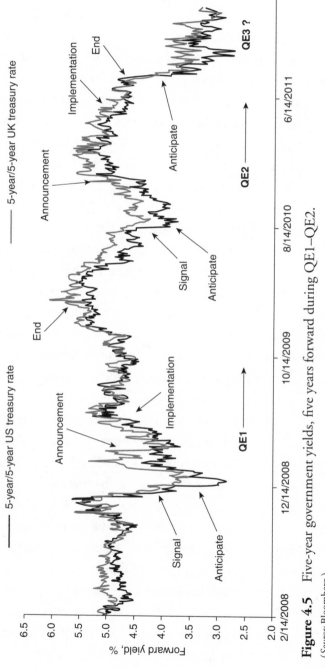

Figure 4.5 Five-year government yields, five years forward during QE1–QE2.

(*Source*: Bloomberg.)

71

is determined by a change in the price of another good. Goods can be complements (i.e., if the price of good A rises more than that of a similar good B, you tend to consume more of the latter) or substitutes (i.e., if the price of good A rises and that increases the demand for good B, which is not a similar good). When a central bank's open market operation leaves its domestic banks with excess money, it also leaves them with excess demand for bonds, which creates the incentive to participate more aggressively in the next government bond auction to complement liquidity. As the demand for liquidity continues, domestic new-issue bond rates are pushed down, perhaps to the point where foreign bonds could become more attractive.

Domestic banks then could seek to substitute foreign new-issue bonds. This is the *third-order effect of QE*—a domestic central bank's excess money generation supports the foreign fiscal authority's budget funding. The fear has been that creating large excess reserves would be inflationary in the near term, whereas in fact it actually tends to be deflationary. The reason is that as the demand elasticity through open market operations increases, it could, through substitution, appreciate the exchange rate of the foreign issuing country. A strong currency may dampen domestic inflation via imports.

This creates *QE's fourth-order effect*—when a central bank creates excess liquidity, it could influence monetary conditions through the exchange rate for the foreign central bank. The foreign central bank could respond by generating its monetary base through (*competitive*) QE, which then leads to the fact that the excess demand for the foreign bank's currency leads partly back to the original central bank's bond market, thereby appreciating its exchange rate. The net effect is that a liquidity preference through cross-border bond demand elasticity leads to exchange-rate stability, thus potentially anchoring price levels (mostly through imports). These QE order effects hold true as long as the liquidity competition is kept fierce by all QE central banks. This type of competition likely could remain an element of the future monetization policies that financial markets could encounter. Thus QE second-, third-, and fourth-order effects are additional financial domino effects that have the objective of growing into economic domino effects. Thus there are different ways to think about QE, and there are different effects. As with monetary transmission, the effects can become compounding, as Figure 4.6 demonstrates.

This figure shows how various versions of QE policy could be divided into different implementation styles and objectives. Another key feature of QE is that it is *temporary*. Thus far, QE programs by the Fed and the Bank of England have an expiration date, and although the extension QE programs have proven to be discretionary, causing a shock in expectations, QE has not been infinite or unlimited. Increasingly, as time went on and deleveraging by the financial, private, and public sectors took on a diverse pattern in terms of speed, QE became creative, as evidenced by Operation Twist (an operation where the Federal Reserve buys longer-maturity Treasury bonds and sells shorter-maturity bonds), as well as being discretionary, contingent on the state of economy, and

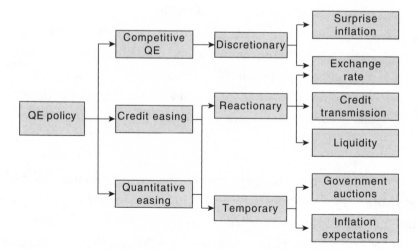

Figure 4.6 QE channels.

even aggressive. In this context, some central banks have been taken a position that places them above the law.

Credit Easing and Risk On/Risk Off

When a central bank adds liquidity to the financial system, that money may not necessarily be transmitted directly into assets. Rather, the liquidity acts as a kind of "insurance" against solvency risk of certain institutions that experienced distress as a result of jump in default expectations. A central bank's credit easing policy can cause a *flight to liquidity*. This is defined as a sudden shift within a portfolio from risky to less risky assets, such as government bonds. A central bank intervention with liquidity has a direct impact on short-term money-market rates, which fall when the supply of liquidity is greater than demand. As it becomes unattractive to hold excess funds in money-market instruments that are very low yielding, the effect can be three-fold:

1. A portfolio balancing occurs where preferences shift from safety to risk-taking, the evidence of *risk on.*
2. A liquidity effect occurs where the presence of abundant funds in the system improves the bid and offer spreads across markets, allowing risk premiums to narrow.
3. A funding shortage by banks and other institutions allows for credit conditions to loosen as banks lower funding charges to each other.

The central bank acts as a market maker to influence distressed asset prices by drenching them in liquidity or by purchasing the contingent assets from third parties. The central bank also acts to prevent bankruptcies by adding more liquidity than needed, and the close connection between illiquidity and insolvency that causes distress then breaks down. An example is when the ECB decided to start term funding operations by offering a three-year long-term refinancing operation (LTRO) to banks in the Euro-zone system. On November 23, 2011, the first signals of the intention to conduct such an operation appeared when "ECB sources" revealed the following: "The central bank is looking into offering banks liquidity over a two-year or even three-year horizon, the sources said, aiming to free up the increasingly blocked interbank money market and give banks more leeway to buy and hold sovereign bonds." In his speech at the Ludwig Erhard Lecture in Berlin on December 15, 2011, ECB President Mario Draghi explained why the ECB decided to enact longer-term financing operations as follows: "The extension of central bank credit provision to very long maturities is meant to give banks a longer horizon in their liquidity planning. It helps them to avoid rebalancing the maturities of their assets and liabilities through a downscaling of longer-term lending." He went on to explain: "Our second measure will allow banks to use loans as collateral with the Euro-system, thereby unfreezing a large portion of bank assets. It should also provide banks with an incentive to abstain from curtailing credit to the economy and to avoid fire sales of other assets on their balance sheets."

Like Federal Reserve Chairman Bernanke, Draghi saw benefits to such policy, phrased as *credit easing*. The effect was material in that it had indeed the follow-on order outlined in points 1 through 3 above: a portfolio balance from risk-free to riskier assets that gave a sense of risk-on in financial markets early in 2012, markedly improved liquidity conditions, and a funding effect. The official statement of benefits to a policy, acting on that policy, and promising to do more can fuel the psychology of risk-taking. When risk-taking gets noticed in the marketplace, other participants follow, either by enticement or by being forced because of a benchmark underweight or short position that needs to be covered. This has a positive effect in which market technical factors feed on one another, but it can spill over into the economy as confidence rises and favorable financing conditions are passed on. In 2009 and 2011, the ECB conducted LTROs that had terms of one and three years, respectively. In 2009, when the ECB conducted one-year LTRO operations, the large sum taken by banks then (442 billion euros) was used by the same banks to purchase government bonds. The idea was to earn carry by borrowing unlimited funds at 1 percent from the ECB, purchase government bonds at 3 to 5 percent, and pledge them to the ECB as collateral. Moreover government bonds then were viewed as safe, and since they were weighted as zero risk by the Bank of International Settlements (BIS), these securities also were used to bolster depleted bank capital buffers, As a result, the government bond carry trade correlated well with the cumulative outstanding LTROs. This changed during 2010–2011, when sovereign risk increased and the relationship broke down. Between November 23, 2011, and early 2012, the second big-term LTRO had a double-sided *knock-on effect*—excess ECB liquidity reduced the solvency risk of Spanish and Italian government bonds by measure of their yield curves "disinverting," and French sovereign credit default swaps (CDS) as well as currency basis swaps (exchange between a floating rate in one currency and a floating rate in another currency) narrowed. Figure 4.7 shows that the Spanish and Italian yield curves steepened dramatically as short-term maturity yields fell more relative to long-term interest rates, making the difference between them wider. When liquidity was added in euros, the supply of euros drove not only the exchange rate lower but also the euro short-term rates relative to U.S. short-term rates. Because sovereign CDS contracts are settled in dollars, the lowering of euro funding costs implied by the exchange rate narrowed the CDS risk premium. Thus the ECB liquidity injection had multiple effects at the same time. The

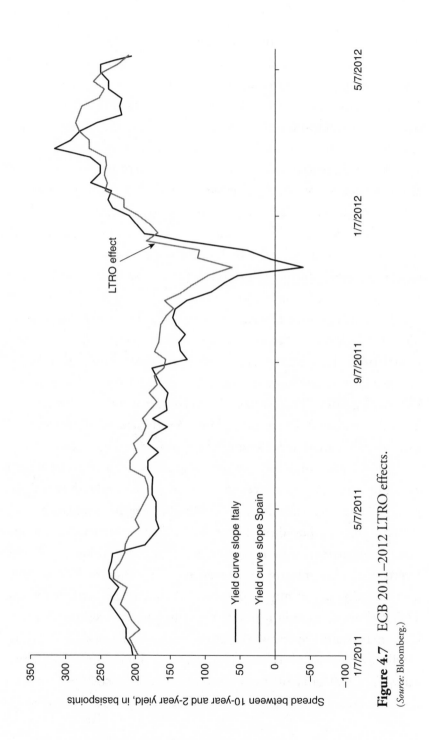

Figure 4.7 ECB 2011–2012 LTRO effects.

(Source: Bloomberg.)

liquidity injection also caused anticipation of carry trades. This effect involves investor anticipation that carry-trade flows into front-end sovereign bonds leads investors to invest in what is deemed to be the "trade du jour" without knowing whether it has in fact occurred. As such, the expectation of flow creates flow, driving bonds up in value, and, like a domino effect, becomes self-reinforcing.

The liquidity also had a broader spillover to other risk assets, such as the Australian dollar, the Standard & Poor's (S&P) 500 Index, the price of crude, and even U.S. Treasury bonds. This created a *risk-on environment.* In general, a risk-on/risk-off environment occurs when asset prices are driven largely by how the appetite for risk advances or retreats over different periods of time. The synchronized way in which this happens across assets and regions tends to be faster than usual, which is a reflection of investors buying and selling riskier assets at the same time, where less attention is paid to the characteristics of the asset. Correlations play a great role, perceived as a "risky jump" when they go to one. As correlations go to one, finance would say that returns and risks of all assets will adjust to such an extent that their risk/return profiles offer the same Sharpe ratio. However, the *law of one price* argues that whenever there is a bargain owing to mispricing, it will be arbitraged even when the securities are not identical. When a central bank adds more liquidity than needed, an arbitrage naturally occurs where participants switch cash holdings into higher-risk-premium assets.

Central bank liquidity injections could spark issuance in the primary bond markets. The reason for this is that as funding conditions improve, the window to issue reopens. This window can be brief because it depends greatly on investors' sentiment and appetite for risk. The level of risk premiums matters greatly, and the liquidity injection has a maximum impact when those premiums are high and market conditions are illiquid. Illiquidity is measured, for example, by the prevailing bid and offer in the market. When the central bank times it well, its signaling and subsequent actions can cause a front-running effect in riskier assets that reignites—that is, the term *risk on*. The ECB three-year LTRO was a good example of risk on.

Above the Law

In 1984, Barro and Gordon simulated how, under credible rules, the monetary authority can exercise significant discretion to generate higher than expected inflation by deceiving the public under the condition of rational expectations. By creating shock inflation, short- and long-term benefits would be created in the form of lower real debt with less distorted taxes and Keynesian-type output expansion if rules are set in place to maintain a maximum level of inflation and money growth. Their framework in particular challenges the question of what the central bank's choice of inflation and unemployment levels will be in the exit scenario to ensure maximized output. Exiting or stay committed to unconventional measures implies a choice of both an inflation rate and an unemployment rate. In essence, QE is about lowering the economy's outstanding balance of money expressed in real terms. By expanding the supply of money at a given demand, the real rate of interest eventually should decline to a point where the level would make the tradeoff of holding bonds (or saving) versus holding money (to spend) zero. This has been argued by both Keynesians and monetarists, whereby the idea of a high (low) real interest rate is the equivalent of a negative (positive) inflation rate. If interest paid on a bond or on money itself is negative, it is not unlikely that the money will be spent on something else rather than being held in bonds or in the bank. With the purchase of assets, real interest rates could be driven lower, which should incentivize bondholders to convert their bonds into money and spend it on goods before their prices become in nominal terms too expensive.

Barro and Gordon argued that the public's incentive to convert bonds into money can be influenced by adjusting the expected real rate of interest and the inflation rate. Under the condition that the public is fully aware of the central bank's plans, there is a temptation to deceive the public by setting an inflation rate that is higher than the rational expectations of inflation rate. One might ask why a central bank would do this and why it would think that it could get away with it. The reason is that in an economic disequilibrium, by setting an inflation rate that exceeds rationally expected inflation, the real interest on debt would be lower, which in the long run should be beneficial to the public in the form of less distorted taxes and output expansion. The central bank could achieve this by increasing the money supply unexpectedly to adjust the expected real interest rate down. This process can continue until the benefit equals the future value loss of overall higher prices when inflation rates cannot be set higher unexpectedly. When this point is reached, the monetary authority should have its hands tied instead of being allowed to freely choose the inflation rate each period. In essence, Barro and Gordon indicate that under a framework of rules, there is significant room for discretion. The reality shows that the concept of temptation (and deception) may not be completely farfetched, as theory suggests. The QE discretionary announcements by the Bank of England and the Fed, for example, had a profound effect on inflation expectations, as Figure 4.8 shows. By announcing QE unexpectedly, a surprise effect in inflation expectations occurred, with the view that future inflation would be allowed to go higher.

The type of discretion taken is connected to a central bank being creative with market positioning—creative even to that extent that a central bank engineers a *short squeeze*. The most famous example involves actions by the Hong Kong Monetary Authority (HKMA) that caused a short squeeze in the Hang Seng Index in 1998. When Hong Kong's financial market was under severe speculative attack during the Asian financial crisis in October 1997, the strategy of the speculators was to bid up Hong Kong's interbank rate and subsequently benefit from large short positions in stock futures. When speculative attacks

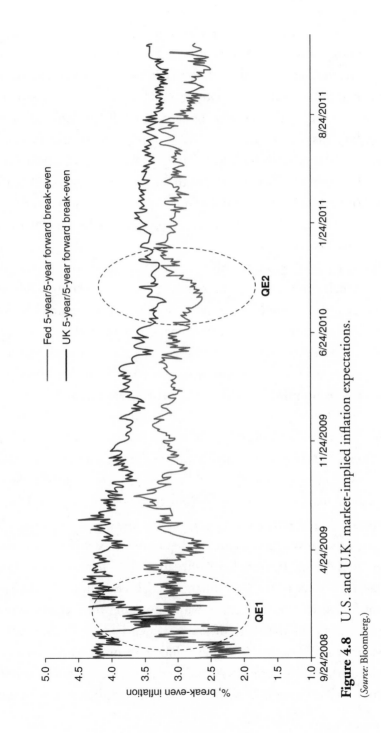

Figure 4.8 U.S. and U.K. market-implied inflation expectations.

(*Source:* Bloomberg.)

continued, the HKMA opted for a stock market intervention. During the last two weeks of August 1998, the HKMA imposed temporary penalty charges on targeted lenders that served as settlement banks for the manipulators and speculators to make speculative funds more expensive, whereas HKMA itself bought $15 billion worth of Hang Seng Index constituent stocks (8 percent of the index's capitalization). In addition, the HKMA took naked long positions that pushed stock futures 20 percent higher to squeeze the naked short sellers. After the intervention, the Hong Kong dollar quickly stabilized, and short-term interest rates normalized. The HKMA succeeded—but not without inflicting pain on investors.

Another more recent example involves the Swiss National Bank (SNB), which on September 6, 2011, released a declaration of war on its exchange currency, the Swiss franc, vis-à-vis the euro. The following is an excerpt of the statement that emphasizes the elements of "war": "With immediate effect, it will no longer tolerate a EUR/CHF exchange rate below the minimum rate of CHF 1.20. The SNB will enforce this minimum rate with the utmost determination and is prepared to buy foreign currency in unlimited quantities."

Prior to this statement, the SNB injected a total of 200 billion Swiss francs (~100 billion dollars) into the Swiss banking system to drive money-market rates drastically lower. The SNB used the Swiss Treasury bill market to repurchase those Swiss francs from banks and employed foreign-exchange swaps. The effect of the exchange rate peg at 1.20 to the euro and injection of liquidity was significant because money-market rates turned sharply negative. The SNB policy was the most aggressive yet in the post–financial crisis era, but surprisingly, it was not followed by other central banks pursuing competitive depreciations. Except for the Bank of Japan, which later in October 2011 intervened with close to 100 billion dollars to prop up the Japanese yen. What the SNB statement does show, however, is that a central bank can take discretion in policy at any time despite statutory limits such as an inflation target. A central bank is also not subject to securities law, but its central bankers are, as the case of SNB former President Hildebrand showed. In this case, Hildebrand's wife transacted in Swiss franc exchange prior to the SNB decision to peg the currency to the euro and sold afterwards for a net profit. Hildebrand had to resign owing to a breach of compliance procedures. That said, the SNB policy of defending its currency peg will not change or its credibility will be destroyed and its balance sheet subjected to severe losses owing to a sharp fall in the Swiss franc.

Official Interventions

Whenever flight to quality becomes extreme, it can reach a threshold for policy makers to react. These are the so-called officially agreed-upon interventions. This was the case, for example, when the Japanese yen (JPY) appreciated in a "flash crash" to a new record low versus the U.S. dollar when there was extreme uncertainty surrounding its Fukushima Dai-Ichi plant that could have seen a nuclear meltdown. Risk aversion gets excessive when such unusual and rare events have an unknown outcome—a *tail*. The appreciation in JPY was caused by domestic institutional and retail investors entering into an amplification reaction to the nuclear situation. They liquidated their short JPY positions quickly to repatriate funds they would need if catastrophe were to hit Japan. The fears of an international repatriation by Japanese investors mounted, and in reaction, the G-7 issued a statement of a "concerted intervention by the United States, the United Kingdom, Canada, and the ECB with the Bank of Japan," the first concerted intervention since 2000:

> In response to recent movements in the exchange rate of the yen associated with the tragic events in Japan, and at the request of the Japanese authorities, the authorities of the United States, the United Kingdom, Canada, and the European Central Bank will join Japan,

on March 18, 2011, in concerted intervention in exchange markets. As we long have stated, excess volatility and disorderly movements in exchange rates have adverse implications for economic and financial stability. We will monitor exchange markets closely and cooperate as appropriate.

The record low on JPY versus the dollar represented a threshold—a limit to stem acceleration from taking hold. What it presented is that G-7 central banks became *market makers of last resort*, influencing prices during distress. The fact was that an ultrastrong Japanese yen would tighten financial conditions not only in Japan but also worldwide as asset prices reacted adversely. In the context of the time, the strength in the yen interfered with the objectives of other central banks, such as inflation targets, price stability, and dual mandates. The yen was a domino effect—its sudden and excessive strength set off a series of reactions in markets, which led to reactions by policy makers, which led to further response by the markets.

A bilateral intervention such as that with the yen in 2011 or the euro in 2000 is a bold measure. It can set a floor (or a cap) for a period of time on an exchange rate because the intervention is backed a by multitude of central banks. A foreign-exchange intervention also can be unilateral, where a central bank acts on its own, such as the SNB and the Bank of Japan (BoJ) did in 2009–2011. The SNB peg to the euro is an extreme version because Swiss interest rates are near zero, so its aggressive language of determination has so far worked to convince markets. The BoJ has intervened unilaterally on numerous occasions, such as in 2003–2004, when its official zero interest-rate policy was in effect to ward off deflation. In the wake of the European debt crisis, in 2010–2011 the BoJ intervened to stem acceleration of appreciation in the JPY. Many foreign-exchange interventions have shown, however, over time that the exchange rate falls below the original point of intervention. It plays into a statement made by former U.S. Treasury Secretary Robert Rubin, who said, "The necessity when intervening in markets is to do so when markets are moving in the desired direction because fighting markets is futile."

As mentioned in the HKMA example earlier, an "effective" central bank intervention strategy is to engineer a *squeeze*. A short squeeze is driven by an obligation to deliver, but a long squeeze is the need to sell into a falling market to cut losses or adhere to margin calls. The risk of a squeeze is likely the highest near pivot points, the level where the market can tip one way or the other. Analogous to an at-the-money option with a very short expiry that has extremely high gamma, near expiry it can end up in or out of the money. A squeeze strategy carries the risk of picking a fight with financial markets.

Fighting markets is a dangerous choice that a central bank could make. It is also a tradeoff—like the decision to allow more inflation for a period of time to not discourage a rise in employment is a tradeoff between jeopardizing the central bank's credibility to fight future inflation and its function to maintain economic stability. The ECB, for example, made such a tradeoff when it started purchasing government bonds in 2010 (see Chapter 7 for a detailed description). At first, the ECB used force in May 2010 by suddenly purchasing large quantities of Greek, Irish, and Portuguese government bonds as part of what was called *market intervention*. The intervention had a random character, and the ECB conducted this through its Securities Market Program (SMP). This program did cause initial squeezes. When the SPM I intervention began on May 10, 2010, the ECB, as reported by dealers, bought 16 billion euros on that day alone, squeezing Greek bond prices 20 points higher. When SPM II started on August 8, 2011, it had a similar albeit less aggressive effect on Italy, where prices jumped 3 to 5 points on 10 billion euro purchases. The SMP has been characterized as a foreign-exchange type of intervention because the ECB randomly went around dealers and (anecdotally) intervened more heavily around pivot points such as 7 percent yield levels. The SMP has been unsuccessful in capping rates because the ECB is unwilling to commit to an unlimited balance sheet. The SMP effect on bond prices followed an almost identical path that it had on the Swiss franc.

This is the foreign exchange intervention sequence:

1. The central bank suddenly intervenes, and exchange rates or asset prices jump—the *prop-up effect.*
2. The central bank intervention makes participants wary, and even without further interventions or minimal interventions, there is an initial *stabilization phase.*
3. The central bank intervention tapers off, and the risk of failure can increase, which ultimately may lead to *another intervention.*

The ECB decided not to pick a fight with markets because purchasing government debt was viewed as something entirely outside the realm of the central bank's founding principles. Initially, the intervention in Greek bonds helped interest rates to stabilize briefly in Greece. Once the ECB reduced the intensity of its purchases, the market belief in the success of stabilization waned, and Greek bond prices started to fall (resulting from, among other factors, the deteriorating Greek economy). Direct interventions, unlike programs such as QE, do not have expiration dates; they stay random to keep the market alert. The discretion taken in policy actions, for good or for bad, can create unexpected effects.

Monetary easing can come in different forms. It can be quantitative, credit, liquidity, and exchange-rate easing. Monetary easing also can be linked to an inflation target. The Bank of Japan's (BoJ's) introduction of a 1 percent inflation goal in 2012 is such an example. In late 2009, the BoJ announced an "understanding" that the midpoint for inflation is 1 percent because the "policy board does not tolerate year-on-year change in the CPI [consumer price index] equal to or below 0 percent." In February 2012, the BoJ surprised everyone by furthering that understanding, stating, "The price stability goal in the medium to long term is in a positive range of 2 percent or lower in terms of the year-on-year rate of change in the CPI and, more specifically, set a goal at 1 percent for the time being." Introducing an inflation target when real rates are high and the national debt load is swollen does just that—it eases sustainability and solvency risks. The Japanese government bond curve responded accordingly by bull steepening, where 5-year bond yields fell relative to 20- to 40-year-maturity bond yields. By introducing an inflation target, the BoJ attempted to bring short- to medium-term real rates down, but in order for the bank to succeed in gaining target credibility, longer-term real rates would have to rise initially and then should fall eventually. If the rise and subsequent fall in real rates occurred in a healthy manner, then future realized inflation eventually might reach 1 percent. The BoJ's decision caused the short-term real rate differential versus the U.S. to narrow, which weakened the Japanese yen, whereas longer-end Japanese government bond rates got more inflation expectation premiums attached.

Presumably, the BoJ, although closely following the Federal Reserve's actions, would want success by having a target that is credible. To gauge the BoJ's success in achieving higher inflation, market participants look at expected real rates measured, for example, by real yields taken from Treasury inflation-protected securities (TIPS) that discount forward in time. Such real yields are called *expected real rates*—the expression by the markets where returns in real terms could be in the years ahead. In the case of Japan, the average expected real yields were around 1 percent. In the context of adopting an inflation target when short-term rates are at zero bound, a real yield well above potential GDP when debt to GDP is large could create greater debt-sustainability risks. Debt sustainability may have been an alternative motive for the BoJ to introduce an inflation target, more so because it implies targeting long-term expected real rates. One could agree that the BoJ is extremely challenged at achieving this, given secular demographics and the strength in its currency. Bank of England's Governor Mervyn King called this at the inflation report press conference in February 2012 the "paradox of policy"—an extraordinarily difficult adjustment where monetary policy may reach a limit. That limit may be rejected or ignored by central banks because monetary easing measures continued to be deployed. An inflation target in the case of Japan eventually may lead to lower real rates. In the case of the United States, the United Kingdom, Germany, and some other countries, though, if the central bank's "reflation" strategy (policy aimed at creating inflation) is successful, long-term real rates have scope to turn positive. The postmortem of the 2008 financial crisis has brought about an aggressive and creative cycle of monetary policy that goes well beyond what central banks are supposed to do. Such policies are meant to facilitate the gigantic debt and financial asset deleveraging with which financial markets and economies have to cope. From a financial domino framework perspective, the unconventional policy actions in response to different crises lead to a multitude of effects through different markets. They may create additional symptoms and aftereffects, which Chapter 5 will discuss.

Chapter 5

Symptoms

There can be symptoms in the aftermath of a financial or sovereign crisis. Some of these are abstract concepts that might have been topics of discussion in academic research that never saw the light of day in financial markets and with policy makers. However, a crisis may change this position materially because the concepts could provide a comprehensive solution or a viable, creative alternative for policy setting. At present, the abstract symptoms that are receiving attention by markets are, for example, financial repression, multiple equilibria, and liquidity traps. The academic debate attempted to quantify their potential effect in a model environment, but now they are becoming reality. Repression, multiple equilibria, and liquidity traps come in different shapes and forms, can be directly visible and measurable, or can be subtle. Whichever way they appear, literature by Carmen Reinhart, Paul de Grauwe, Paul Krugman, and others has shown that such symptoms can have lasting consequences for the functioning of economies and financial markets. The much-cited and most vivid example is Japan, which, after its real estate bubble burst, employed forms of financial repression and has been mired in a liquidity trap. This was a direct result of a balance sheet recession.

A *balance sheet recession* occurs when a bubble implodes, and investors start rationally valuing assets based on a *discounted cash flow* (DCF) method to properly reflect fundamentals. The method values future free cash flow by discounted present values at a weighted-average cost of capital. Whatever value is spit out that is higher than the original cost presents an opportunity for investment. When there is a shift from the irrational to the rational, a deleveraging force sets in subsequently. Even with interest rates near zero, a tradeoff is made in favor of debt minimization versus profit maximization. Richard Koo describes this deleveraging as the "yang yin cycle" of effective (yang) and ineffective (yin) monetary policy. In the yin part of the cycle, asset purchases (quantitative easing [QE]) are not effective because the program has an expiration date, the central bank is seen as not a permanent holder of the assets because it doesn't want to take excessive risk beyond its realm, and purchases will be rationally evaluated under the DCF method. Since asset purchases and stock held by the central bank are seen being temporary, the DCF method is likely to deflate propped-up asset values as debt paydowns continue. Richard Koo's conclusion is that unless a central bank turns absolutely mad, any type of nonstandard monetary policy is just liquidity injections.

At a juncture where global monetary and fiscal policy appear perhaps to be ineffective, the "discounted value of expectations of future earnings," as discussed by Bridgewater Ray Dalio, can no longer be used. By artificially driving confidence higher by propping up asset values through QE, borrowing behavior continues to be discouraged when debt levels stay elevated. The *present-value effect* of assets that enables borrowing and spending has run into a wall even if central banks would aim to slash longer-term rates toward zero. As the DCF method explains, when a longer period of time is needed to bring future values back to present values, a risk premium is added to the discount rate as compensation for cash flow not materializing after all. The potential buyers rationally value the banks' assets at lower values because previously they have been at inflated levels. A balance sheet recession can spill over to other healthy balance sheets. Balance sheet recessions can provoke a *corner solution*. To end deleveraging in a meaningful way, either (1) aggressive global debt monetization or (2) widespread sovereign and private-sector debt restructurings/ defaults may commence. But both solutions don't come without symptoms. Debt monetization may happen directly via the central bank or indirectly via regulatory or other "forced" methods. This kind of monetization can fall under repression, but it also results in a liquidity-type trap as a reaction by a central bank to end it. As Figure 5.1 shows, U.S. debt to gross domestic product (GDP) ratios measured against real policy rates may push corner solutions to facilitate deleveraging. However, each major central bank can choose to do this with discretion and in a particular way.

There is also a connection in which financial repression may lead in some markets to lower nominal bond yields than others, and the difference in bond yields effectively creates multiple equilibria. Lower nominal bond yields also can be driven by a liquidity trap. If repression forces yields down through regulatory approaches that require the holding of government bonds, liquidity traps mirror low inflation and growth expectations that can drive government bond yields and other rates lower. Thus, since repression, multiple equilibria, and liquidity traps are unique "abstract" and standalone factors, they can happen simultaneously, and they can be connected. Like dominoes, they may complement each other or serve as a catalyst. The following sections explain the concepts in further detail.

Symptom One: Financial Repression

Carmen Reinhart published a paper on financial repression titled, "The Liquidation of Government Debt." In this paper she discussed how financial repression occurs and the strong connection between

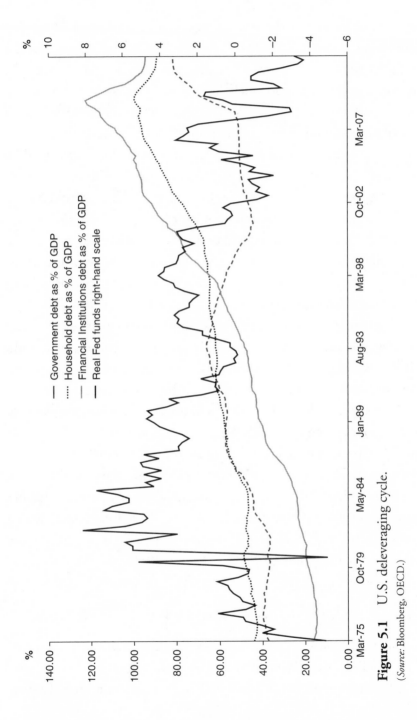

Figure 5.1 U.S. deleveraging cycle.

(*Source:* Bloomberg, OECD.)

92

times of repression and high inflation. Carmen Reinhart sees the following factors as a cause for financial repression:

1. Explicit or indirect caps or ceilings on interest rates sponsored by the government
2. A captive audience maintained by capital account restrictions, reserve requirements, or prudent regulatory measures
3. Direct ownership by domestic institutions

These factors generate a structural demand for government debt, which creates a disconnect between very low nominal bond yields and higher inflation. The disconnect allows for what Reinhart calls a "stealth liquidation" of government debt. Her empirical research shows that a large number of countries after World War II have been able to benefit from such a method to reduce government debt via indirect taxation, namely, a financial repression tax. Noteworthy from Reinhart's research results is that the countries that followed the course of repression were able to liquidate their government debt over an average time span of 35 years, with inflation of 6 to 8 percent, negative real rates of 3.5 percent, and number of liquidation years as 9. A *liquidation year* is defined as a year when (short-term) real rates stay consistently negative. Reinhart also defines a *debt-reduction period* as any decline in the debt-to-GDP ratio over a three-year window (albeit not specified in percentage terms). When measured against inflation performance during those years, it turns out that inflation is higher during debt-reduction years than otherwise. And, because real rates stay negative, the savings to the government is the *liquidation effect* or *financial repression tax*—negative real rate times the total outstanding government debt stock (plus price return).

Figure 5.2 shows real T-bill rates for major countries and Greece. Strictly speaking, most T-bill real rates turned negative by late 2009, so most countries experienced two years of liquidation. Debt-to-GDP

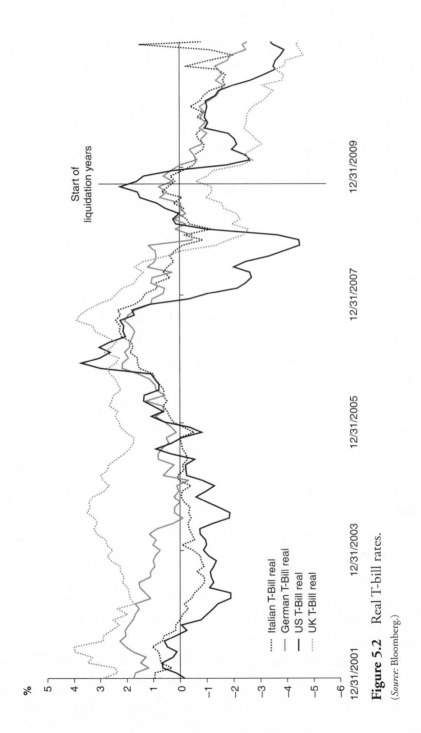

Figure 5.2 Real T-bill rates.

(*Source:* Bloomberg.)

94

ratios, however, have increased rather than decreased since that time. Thus, although low nominal rates are disconnected from higher (headline) inflation, so is current liquidation from debt-reduction years. Following Reinhart's definition of repression, where negative real rates and debt reduction go hand in hand, officially we may not yet be in such a period. If Reinhart is correct, once a period of repression is entered, nominal rates stay low because they are capped one way or another. Reinhart acknowledges in her conclusion that forms of repression are under way in Europe, where debt is placed below market rates in pension funds and financial institutions. U.S. and U.K. institutions have increased government bond holdings, and that has been a trend since the middle of 2007. Quantitative easing (QE) and anchored-policy-rate strategies have brought in nonmarket players that have changed the price setting of government bonds. Then there are small signs of Italian and Belgian debt management offices targeting the retail segment with incentives to buy domestic government bonds. There is also anecdotal evidence of moral suasion, where banks and primary dealers are 'incentivized" to bid on government bonds.

The implication of liquidation in nonrepression years is that having a debt overhang of varying degrees among households, institutions, and governments will cause debt reduction to be intensely focused on alternative methods. These alternatives are basically (1) a debt snowball (accelerated debt payoff), (2) default via reprofiling, rescheduling, voluntary rollover, or hard restructuring, and (3) surprise inflation. Reinhart's study shows that liquidation years for the majority are shared with episodes of surprise inflation (inflation is 2 standard deviations above a 10-year moving average).

Once more, alternative methods can create domino effects. A "debt snowball" may cause tightening of financial conditions in such a way that it adversely affects solvency conditions for individuals, companies, and governments. This could lead to such methods as reprofiling or rescheduling (maturity extension) of government debt that may cause longer-term inflation expectations to rise. An important finding from Reinhart's research is that when liquidation years (years when real rates stay negative) fall together with debt-reduction years, a sudden burst of inflation may occur. As financial markets travel toward a repression era, inflation expectations are likely to stay elevated. If they do not, they become unanchored.

Because repression is associated with real interest rates, theories, such as those by Knutt Wicksell in his work *Interest and Prices* (1898), may be relevant. In his book, Wicksel argues that there is an equilibrium for interest rates, which he called the "natural real rate of interest." Wicksell said that this rate is a "certain rate of interest on loans which is neutral in respect to commodity prices and tends neither to raise nor to lower them." The natural interest rate is unobservable but could be approximated by real potential GDP under the condition that long-term inflation expectations are stable. Real potential GDP is in economic terms the same as the output gap, the difference between actual production and a long-term average. In this context, the natural rate of interest also can be enamored of the long-run average of the central bank rate in real terms. The basic idea of Wicksell's theory is that when current real rates are below the natural real rate, monetary policy is very accommodative. Such accommodation plays a role in financial repression as well. If there is ongoing price inflation, numerous government interventions to set interest rates and direct the flow of credit shrink the deposit base for domestic bank lending, allowing for monetary policy to remain tolerant of inflation. And since financial repression is motivated by fiscal needs, measures such as high reserve and liquidity ratio requirements or interest ceilings make savers usually unaware of such policies because they are not made known publicly. Savers therefore face low nominal rates on bonds and deposits that are aggravated by rising inflation—hence real rates turn negative and become repressive.

There is an argument to be made that since there is an unobservable natural real rate, there also could be an unobservable *natural real rate of repression.* This rate is the extreme form of repression when a government can succeed consistently with repressive policies. The success of such policies is based on an unobservable real rate of repression unknown to the public. Carmen Reinhart noted that when real rates stay persistently below the actual real GDP growth rate, this allows for drastic reductions in government debt. Reinhart's argument can be extended to the concept of a natural real rate of repression. When a central bank real rate is below real potential GDP (measured by the output gap in real terms), the difference shows how repressive monetary policy really is. In comparing the real policy rate with the output gap for the United States, the United Kingdom, and Germany, it is striking is that in all three countries the real policy rate is above the real output gap. According to the Organisation for Economic Co-ordination and Development (OECD) Economic Outlook Annex, the 2012 output gap for the United States and the United Kingdom is about 4 percent, whereas for Germany it is 1.7 percent. The real policy rates in the United States, the United Kingdom, and Germany are around −1.5 percent (adjusted for 2012 headline inflation).

This may imply the following: The real policy rates have been negative since 2008 and below actual real GDP, but they are nowhere near extreme forms of repression. Since the output gap in real terms is very negative, the central banks of, namely, the United States and the United Kingdom are quite likely to have to remain accommodative for a longer period of time, allowing for both governments to potentially succeed with extreme forms of repression. Germany's difference between real policy rate and output gap is the narrowest of the three. However, tighter monetary policy also can entice a form of repression. Along these lines, we can analyze two recent cases in markets.

When the European Central Bank (ECB) began "normalization" of its policy stance in the summer of 2010 and subsequently hiked in

April 2011, Greek, Irish, and Portuguese two-year government bond yields skyrocketed, reaching 10 percent to as high as 25 percent. This was caused in part by the tightened financial conditions resulting from higher interest rates and in part, as described in Chapters 4 and 5, by the market forced austerity measures stemming from the domino effect of the Euro-zone debt crisis. The market distress shut down capital market funding for all three countries, and as a result, the ECB tightened monetary policy, which repressed Greek, Irish, and Portuguese domestic banks into their domestic treasury bills. As financial conditions tightened and funding in capital and wholesale markets dried up, the Greek and Portuguese banks had no other alternative than to purchase treasury bills from their own treasuries and use those as collateral to access funding at the ECB or their national central bank via emergency liquidity assistance (ELA), the only two sources of funding that were left. The effect has been that although two-year government bond yields are 50 percent positive in real terms, the treasury bill yields turned negative in real terms, as shown Figure 5.3. This is a form of *tightening repression*—a central bank that makes a tradeoff between inflation and default for the sake of its independence and credibility.

Tightening repression also resulted in explicit statements by, for example, the Italian treasury on December 27, 2011. Part of the statement is as follows:

> 2012 will see the Treasury very active with money market instruments, such as three-month or non-standard maturity ("flexible") BOTs [Italian short-term bonds], Commercial Papers and Treasury Operations (OPTES) in order to offset temporary cash imbalances. Issuance activity of BOTs will continue to be with the traditional 3-, 6- and 12-month maturities, but these may be supported by flexible maturities for liquidity management purposes.

The intensity of the Euro debt crisis caused high volatility in Italian government bonds. It caused the Italian treasury to become more proactive and creative with its large refunding program scheduled for

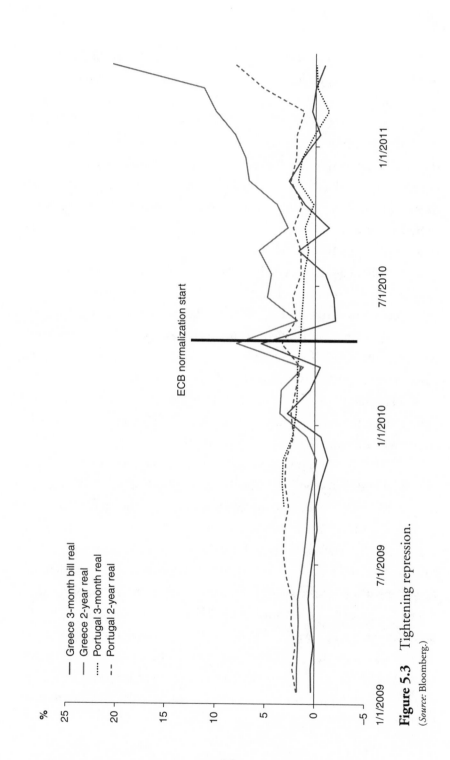

Figure 5.3 Tightening repression.

(*Source:* Bloomberg.)

99

2012. The statement presented incentives such as dealers being allowed to place more bids in auctions on behalf of clients, the exploration of a retail Italian government bond to target buy-and-hold-to-maturity domestic investors, and a focus on the shorter end of the Italian yield curve, where interest rates are, on average, 1 to 3 percent lower than those for longer-maturity Italian bonds. Italian banks would purchase especially treasury bills as collateral for funding at the ECB. The statement and the incentives the Italian treasury presented could be interpreted as a form of repression. That said, because repression is subtle, such an interpretation is subjective.

The other case is so-called currency repression. A central bank can ease financial conditions via rate cuts, purchases from the private sector, or currency interventions. When inflation is rising but production capacity remains constrained, sometimes devaluing the currency is a logical easing choice for a central bank in order to maintain credibility. There have explicit cases of this, such as the recent currency peg the Swiss National Bank (SNB) set at 1.20 to the euro in order to ward off deflationary pressure stemming from excessive strength in the Swiss franc, which again resulted from capital flight during the Euro debt crisis. In the case of the United States, the results of consistent accommodative monetary policy since the early 2000s have been dramatic for the dollar. As the Fed expanded its monetary policy far into unconventional territory, the real funds rate fell further below the natural real rate. Figure 5.4 shows that each time this occurred, there was a precipitous decline in the dollar. A currency thus becomes repressive when the negative real rate differential is forced on other countries. Since their higher positive real rates attract large capital inflows into their domestic bond markets and a weakening of the dollar drives commodity prices up, this adversely drives up inflation rates in countries with higher real rates. As a result, more counter monetary reaction via tightening policies, as well as capital controls, drives up real interest rate differentials further.

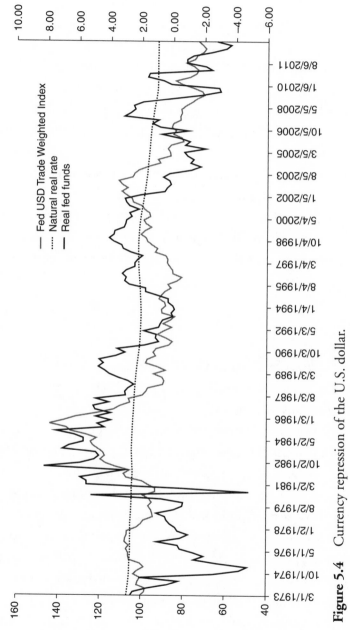

Figure 5.4 Currency repression of the U.S. dollar.
(*Source:* Bloomberg.)

101

As Figure 5.4 shows, today, the real fed funds rate is about 4 percent below the natural real rate but still not as extreme as during the early 1970s, when the difference was 6 percent. As noted by Carmen Reinhart, when the difference is large, it allows for a stealth liquidation of debt aided by a central bank not committed to a stronger currency. Hence a policy to implicitly weaken the currency could be repressive when other countries experience capital inflows as a result. As long as countries tolerate such a policy, it falls under the umbrella of a stealth or subtle approach. When it gets noticed because the adverse effects show up in the form of inflation, it gets stipulated as "beggar thy neighbor" deliberate currency policy. The policy reaction that may occur is a round of competitive devaluations that end the currency repression tactic. When this happens, domino effects quickly occur in markets because depreciating currencies also affect commodity, bond, and equity markets.

Symptom Two: Multiple Equilibria

In a *Financial Times* op-ed in October 2011, economist Erik Nielsen compared Italy and U.K. government debt. Nielsen's conclusion was that the Italian government can fund itself at a 5.5 to 6 percent interest rates despite having a net investment position (net debt to foreign creditors) at −24 percent of GDP and a primary surplus position at 0.9 percent of GDP. The U.K. government, on the other hand, has the luxury of obtaining funding at around 3 percent, yet the United Kingdom has a worse net investment position (−13 percent) and a greater primary deficit (−5 percent). The difference in funding rates can be explained by two factors: (1) the currency and (2) the ability to print and control the currency in which the domestic debt is issued and denominated. For the United Kingdom, the debt issued in pounds sterling (GBP) also can be issued by a lender of last resort, the Bank of England. In Europe, there is a lender of last resort—the ECB—but individual countries cannot independently "print" the euro. As a result, there is also within Europe funding differences between, for example, Italy at higher (5 to 6 percent) versus Germany at lower rates (2 to 3 percent).

This difference has been termed *multiple equilibria*—a phenomenon where a country issues debt in a currency it can't print in unlimited fashion and therefore has no control over. Such is the case for certain emerging-market debt that succumbs to occasional defaults because the countries borrow in currencies (mainly dollars) that they cannot print. When this is recognized by markets, the tolerance for public finances of such countries is far, far less. Multiple equilibria typically are caused by the absence of a lender of last resort. In the Euro zone, this is a unique situation because the ECB, composed of 17 national central banks that in essence can function as lenders of last resort, is perhaps not fully present for every country. This is evident from the ECB bond purchase program (SMP), which buys debt only from a select group of countries, whereas presumably it could buy debt from all Euro-zone countries. In the United Kingdom, there is no discrimination of this kind because the Bank of England (BoE) can purchase all the debt denominated in its own currency.

In an analysis by the Bank Credit Analyst (BCA) Research, a diagram was presented to illustrate the dynamics of the European debt crisis (Figure 5.5). Since speculative attacks occur in a crisis, the distinction between liquidity and solvency diminishes. As such, the supply and demand for bonds may create several equilibrium yields, a reflection of shifts in debt-to-GDP ratios between the different markets. The figure shows a downward-sloping curve as demand for bonds rises when prices fall (yields rise). At a certain level in yields, the demand psychology can suddenly change as insolvency is called into question. BCA Research called it the "vulnerability zone" (see gray area in Figure 5.5), the area where the demand curve (snakelike curve) becomes upward-sloping; that is, bond prices have to go down a lot further before demand will normalize (downward-sloping lower

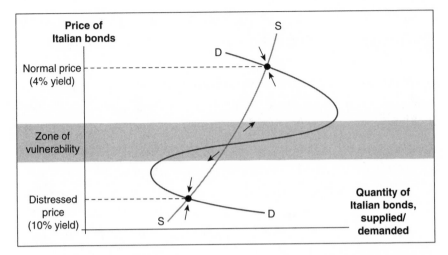

Figure 5.5   BCA Research illustration of multiple equilibria: When a lender of last resort is absent, multiple equilibria are possible.

(*Source:* © BCA Research 2011, www.bcaresearch.com)

end of Figure 5.5). The gist is that the figure shows two equilibria, both where supply and demand functions are normal but at different prices.

   Another explanation has been given by University of Leuven's Paul de Grauwe, who defined "good" and "bad" equilibria. Bad equilibria are defined as a solvency shock that is a sharp fall in government revenues as a result of recession. De Grauwe compared this to the benefit and incentive to default. There is a cost and a benefit to default—the benefit of expected and unexpected default and the cost of reputation loss and inability to borrow in the future by the government that defaults. The larger the solvency shock, the greater is the benefit because the incentive is very high for a government to default. There are two types of default curves: the benefit curve when default is anticipated and the benefit curve when default is not anticipated. The cost of default is assumed to be fixed, but there is a degree of solvency shock from small to intermediate to large. De Grauwe suggests that the solvency shock arrives at two equilibria. One is where the default is expected and so the benefits outweigh the cost, which can give a government an incentive to default. The other is where default is not expected and the benefits are below the cost, so the government is less likely to default. De Grauwe names these "bad equilibrium" and "good equilibrium."

Good and bad equilibria were first identified by French economist Léon Walras, who in *Elements of Pure Economics* established the foundation for what became known as the *general equilibrium theory*. In this theory, the behavior of supply, demand, and prices is central in a whole economy with several or many interacting markets, and this is shown by seeking to prove that a set of prices exists that will result in an overall equilibrium, hence a *general equilibrium* in contrast to a *partial equilibrium*, which only analyzes single markets. General equilibrium is also known as the *bottom-up approach*. Good and bad equilibria also can be further specified in financial market terms. A bad equilibrium is characterized by excessive flight to quality, steep yield curves, high volatility across asset classes, and intense, creative monetary policy actions. A good equilibrium would see policy makers in control of markets, effective monetary policy, deleveraging ends, and a healthy level of inflation expectations return. Markets can bounce between both equilibria, often cited as *risk-on* and *risk-off days*. There is also an element of *tipping*, where the market falls suddenly from risk-on to risk-off on the same day. This is identified with domino effects that under unexpected causality can result in a good or a bad equilibrium.

Today, multiple equilibria are especially visible in the European government bond markets. Underlying this is the theoretical backdrop to multiple equilibria. Countries that join a monetary union give up control of their currency. These countries issue government debt in a currency over which they do not have control. The result is that the governments cannot guarantee that cash will be available for bondholders to claim. Countries outside a monetary union that have their own central banks can ensure that bondholders will be paid at maturity because the central bank always can print currency. When a liquidity crisis happens in a monetary union and interest rates on government debt rise, a government can face the potential of a default. This dynamic has a self-fulfilling nature: Investors fear default and sell their bonds, more investors react, and in the absence of a central bank intervention, a liquidity crisis degenerates into a solvency crisis. As the self-full filling prophecy says: Fear of insolvency creates conditions that make insolvency more likely. The dislocation is perhaps most severe in the inflation-linked government bond market. This difference in real interest rates reflects the wide outcomes associated with good and bad equilibria, namely, inflation (Germany, negative real yield) and deflation (Italy, positive real yield). The difference also shows how sovereign credit risk shifts after a financial crisis. Before the 2008 financial crisis, the differentiation between emerging and developed market interest rates was made on the basis of *credit risk* versus *interest-rate risk*. Today that differentiation continues to exist, although a marked "convergence" between the two types of risk has happened within the global bond universe. Figure 5.6 shows that the interest-rate differences were wide among developed and emerging markets during the financial crisis. This wideness has remained in place, but a shift has occurred involving countries that were initially deemed as at interest-rate risk, but are now perceived to have higher credit risk. Beneath the surface are factors such as credit ratings migration, liquidity, solvency, and central bank intervention via unconventional measures. This caused a demand shift out of certain government bonds by end investors, creating the notion of multiple equilibria, the different levels of interest rates that reflect different levels of debt relative to GDP. The figure also shows how emerging countries such as Mexico have an interest-rate level that is closer to that of Italy because Mexico's rating (BBB+) is lower than Italy's (A–), but there is big difference between the two countries' debt-to-GDP ratio—36 percent for Mexico and 120 percent for Italy.

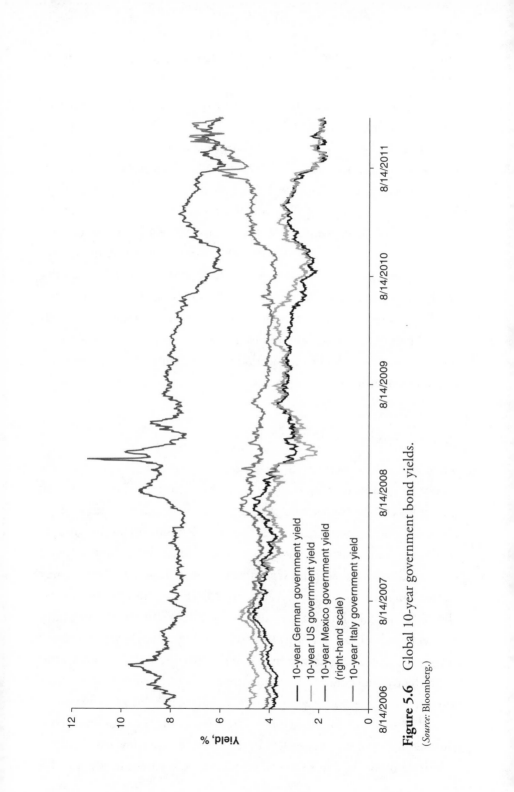

Figure 5.6 Global 10-year government bond yields.

(*Source:* Bloomberg.)

There is also an element of flight to quality or liquidity, whereas interest rates in the United Kingdom are well below those of Spain, even though the UK's debt-to-GDP ratio is higher (85 percent) than that of Spain (66 percent). Whenever the risk of liquidity and solvency are in close proximity, the yield differences reflect each other in their own equilibrium, meeting demand at a different price. Since liquidity versus solvency has created a level of distress in global markets, central banks have become an increasingly more dominant demand factor for government bonds, bringing yields lower and thereby masking worsening debt metrics for certain markets such as the United States. Figure 5.6 presents a different interest-rate spectrum from that which existed before the crisis, where liquidity and solvency factors played a greater role than a traditional outlook on fundamentals such as inflation and unemployment.

Symptom Three: Liquidity Traps

There are several definitions of a *liquidity trap*. The Keynesian version says a liquidity trap occurs when the effectiveness of monetary policy is zero. In such a case, demand for money doesn't respond to the low level of interest rates because the demand for money is perfectly elastic. In basic supply/demand diagrams, the money demand curve is downward-sloping (as interest rates fall, demand for money should increase), but conceivably, in a liquidity trap environment, the curve is flat. The classic version by Hicks says that a liquidity trap is based on expectations of future money supply. When money supply is kept static, the money supply curve remains vertical, that is, perfectly inelastic. A demand-driven liquidity trap, traditionally known as a *Keynesian liquidity trap*, occurs when bond yields reach a level at or close to the interest rate earned on the monetary base (interest on excess reserves). The demand for money can become infinitely inelastic. No matter how low interest rates are, the private sector's demand for money to invest and spend has become insensitive to the level of interest rates.

A liquidity trap influenced by central bank money is a supply-driven liquidity trap. In such a liquidity trap, money supply could become inelastic in relation to interest rates when the substitution effect between risk and less riskier assets disappears as future supplied central bank money is not fully replaced by the private sector. When a central bank keeps liquidity fixed, the side effect may be a trap in which the private sector finds itself in a situation where excess liquidity gets reinvested into government bonds and stays there. This effect is accentuated by the preferred habitat of investors who prefer a certain segment of the yield curve. When demand for money becomes inelastic, the demand curve should be flat, and when the money supply is inelastic, the supply curve should be horizontal. Somewhere the Keynesian and classic versions of a liquidity trap would intersect theoretically. This would be at a nominal rate where, conceivably, the liquidity trap may become indefinite. Figure 5.7 demonstrates this visually. Before the crisis, presumably the demand for money was more sensitive to interest rates because it was then the main monetary policy tool to influence financial conditions in an economy. After the financial crisis, this changed owing to near-zero rates, so the money demand curve could have become flatter, that is, less sensitive to interest rates. When plotting in this figure the money demand curves before and after the crisis versus five-year U.S. Treasury yields (vertical axis) against short-term inflation expectations (horizontal axis), the scatter plot shows how the five-year Treasury travels more to the left on the graph as inflation expectations fall. If liquidity is trapped with money demand that is insensitive to interest rates, government bond yields will go lower and lower until they reach a point at which they reflect expectations of a potentially permanent liquidity trap.

Associated with liquidity traps are *inflation expectations.* Keynes, Hicks, and Woodford all argued that once an economy enters a liquidity trap, deflation expectations can become entrenched. Of concern,

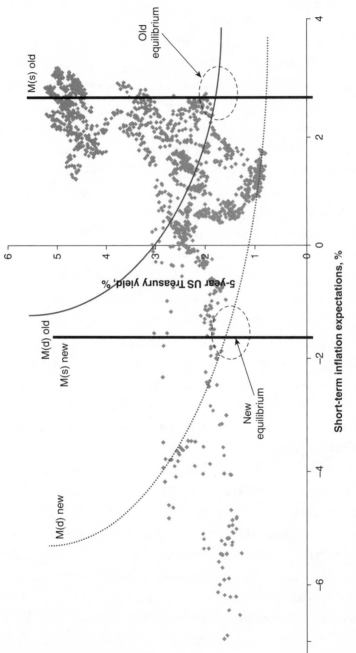

Figure 5.7 The intersection between money demand and supply in a liquidity trap.
(*Source*: Bloomberg.)

then, is how long such a trap may last. The duration of a liquidity trap has a relationship with expected returns. If returns are expected to be negative in real terms, the tradeoff between keeping cash in bonds or other assets versus keeping cash in a mattress or wallet is effectively zero. If such a situation persists, then liquidity will be trapped in an environment of no or limited returns. The only meaningful source of market return would be the slope of the yield curve. The case of Japan has been very striking. If you had invested in a 30-year Japanese government bond in 2001, the annualized return would have been 3 percent versus Japan's stock market, the Nikkei, that delivered −18 percent annualized returns according to Bloomberg data. This was coined the *lost decade*. Paul Krugman gave Japan advice in 1998 to get out of the deflation spiral. He said: "The way to make monetary policy effective is for the central bank to credibly promise to be irresponsible, to make a persuasive case that it will permit inflation to occur, thereby producing the negative real interest rates the economy needs." At present, the Japanese economy remains mired in a liquidity trap.

Deflation is a credibility problem if one instrument is left (fed funds at 0 percent for 10 years). Setting inflation higher as a target, where inflation is today, may bring expectations out of deflation. Reality is that a liquidity trap is hard to spot. Economists would argue that a liquidity trap's characteristics would be a combination of low money growth and velocity, higher savings, and lack of confidence. There could be market-implied measures that may indicate the presence of a trap, for example, comparing short-term implied future yields with long-term bond yields in real terms. Japan may have entered a liquidity trap in the fall of 1997, when 10-year nominal Japanese government bond yields fell below 1 percent and deflation turned real yields into positive territory. A reason is that once Japanese monetary policy became "passive," a shift was made toward fiscal policy. The idea was short-term stimulus versus long-term austerity. Passive monetary policy is characterized by applying communication measures such as extended terms to keep the policy rate unchanged. After the financial crisis, financial markets increasingly feared the potential of multiple liquidity traps in the United States and Europe. In forward interest-rate markets, such liquidity-trap expectations became more visible, where short-term interest-rate expectations for most of the major central bank policy rates remain close to zero for the next two to three years. Since the financial crisis, central bank balance sheets have increased dramatically, but so have their deposit facilities, where commercial banks park excess cash. Despite dramatic monetary easing, the supply-driven liquidity trap became very real. The economics of earning 25 basis points on excess reserves or cash on deposit appear to outweigh the benefits of reinvesting the funds into other assets or lending them out. At the same time, private-sector deleveraging has continued in most major economies despite record low borrowing rates. These dynamics have led to a not-seen-before combination of both a demand and supply–type liquidity trap, a reflection of potential bimodal outcomes. Such an outcome is unlike a typical bell-shaped curve of statistical likelihood, with a single peak and low-probability tails on either side. A flatter or even bimodal (dual-peaked) distribution suggests greater uncertainty over the range of potential outcomes, including extremes called *fat tails* that may be more likely to occur. The differences in the degree to which each central bank holds excess reserves demonstrate that the liquidity trap is not even: Some central banks have been more aggressive in providing liquidity (e.g., the Swiss National Bank) than others, whereas some central banks are just catching up (e.g., the ECB). At an uneven speed of private and financial sector deleveraging, global central banks have to guard against additional traps materializing. Although there was credit creation in the United States over the last few years, the risk of a credit crunch in Europe remains high and could serve as fuel for a global liquidity trap. This may require even more provocative forms of monetary easing, whereby central banks perhaps could end up lending directly to the real economy without bank intermediation. This would be the tipping point for the liquidity trap to dissolve into a potential bout of inflation. This is also where a liquidity trap can meet financial repression. In the last three years, most major central banks have maintained the lower zero bound on their policy rates. This zero bound is seen as a constraint; it sets limits to what a policy maker can do with normal policy tools. The zero bound instead has moved central banks into deploying creative and different types of tools. The zero bound also brings in another limit—the ability to hold cash riskless. Holding cash is not risk-free because it can be destroyed, lost, or stolen. The fee paid for holding a deposit is a tradeoff people are willing to make over holding cash, so paying a low or even negative nominal rate on a Treasury bill or deposit is in this context a convenience.

This kind of psychology plays for banks as well. A bank can profit from borrowing low-cost funds (taking deposits) and relending or reinvesting those funds at a higher rate. The difference between relending and reinvesting is subtle at the zero bound. On one hand, a bank could use the near-zero central bank funds and deploy them into higher-returning assets or lend them to the private sector. On the other hand, a bank could deposit the funds right back at the central bank, which is what has happened in the United States, the United Kingdom, Europe, and Japan since 2008. In general, a bank would earn negative carry this way through quantitative easing (QE) in the United States and the United Kingdom, where banks sell higher-yielding Treasury bonds to the central bank and in return redeposit the funds at the lower (effective) policy rate. In Europe, it is the reverse: Banks borrow at a higher policy rate and return the funds at the lower deposit rate. In both cases, the negative carry earned is again a convenience, a safeguard against holding cash, which is seen as too expensive. The behavior toward depositors from a central bank to a bank or from a bank to an individual is about willingness to relend rather than reinvest. Normally, low deposit rates reflect less default risk, more so because a government guarantee is attached to them (deposit insurance). However, when nominal bond or bill yields are very low or even negative, deposit rates are correspondingly low because banks are likely unwilling to pay depositors high rates when the expected return on loans and other investments is low. At the same time, investors are willing to accept a negative nominal return on a risk-free asset because holding it is cheaper and less risky than transporting and storing cash. There is an incentive to hold cash on deposit that makes the demand for money inelastic to the level of interest rates. When this happens, Keynes judged that the economy is in a liquidity trap. It has been happening at banks and private levels, a reason why credit in the developed world has contracted since the financial crisis. As explained earlier, there are a number of opinions about what a liquidity trap could look like and, above all, how it might relate to the natural rate of interest, the level where interest rates are neutral irrespective of inflation. The neutral rate also could be viewed as a static rate, a rate that is floored by official intervention. In this context with a near-zero policy rate for some time to come, this rate also could be called the *natural (real) interest rate*. Paul Krugman wrote in December 2011 in a *New York Times* op-ed that the near-zero interest rate is not a price ceiling but rather a price floor because people always can hold cash. This could be challenged because the concept of a zero-bound rate can be seen as the opposite; it may discourage people and banks from holding cash but rather encourage them to deposit it at a safeguarded institution, the central bank. Although the zero-bound policy rate cannot turn negative, the implied policy rate by, for example, the Taylor model has been negative since 2008. This negative model–implied policy rate means that there is a mismatch between savings and investment as a consequence of the *re*lending (putting on deposit) behavior. And so the natural rate as in the policy rate, as in the zero-bound rate, is effectively negative. The negative Taylor model–implied rate as well as the negative real fed funds rate is below the natural rate (as estimated by OECD's potential U.S. GDP). The same trend has happened for the United Kingdom, Europe, and Japan, whereas the real and implied policy rates are below their potential GDP (1.2 percent for the United Kingdom, 1 percent for Europe, and 0.7 percent for Japan). The difference between the natural rate and the negative nominal and real rates may continue to entice deposit behavior, challenging the efficacy of monetary policy—all this while the concern remains that the real policy rate will become the equal of prevailing inflation expectations that turn negative. If this were to happen, the real policy rate might turn much higher than the natural rate. This could create the possibility of an unstable dynamic—an excessively high real rate leading to a downward spiral of lower prices that, in turn, raise the real short-term interest rate, which depresses activity and prices further, and so on. In such an environment, deposit outflows should be very high. And it is not fully surprising in the Euro-zone periphery, where the average real short-term rate is above the potential GDP/natural rate (0.7 percent average), that bank deposit outflows have been sharply on the rise over the past few years since the debt crisis began. In response, as the LTRO effect described in Chapter 4, European banks on the periphery continued to use the negative real ECB policy rate of −1.5 percent to borrow and kept placing it at a safe institution, named the ECB, to compensate for their own deposit outflows.

Symptom Four: Riskier-Free Rates

Gillian Tett posed a few good questions in her *Financial Times* op-ed on September 1, 2011:

1. Are U.S. Treasuries still risk-free?
2. Is the concept of a risk-free rate appropriate in today's world?
3. If there is no risk-free rate, what does it mean for portfolio theory and the capital asset pricing model (CAPM)?

In her answers, Tett sought an optimum anchor that represents the "new" risk-free rate. Theoretically, the risk-free rate is the boundary of an investment with no loss. Alternatives to a riskless rate of return could be hard assets such as gold that have no depreciation attached to them. The assumption as to why a rate of return is risk-free is that there is no or little possibility of a government default. And in a flat currency–based system, the government can print unlimited currency to pay debts. Thus, in essence, the risk-free rate reflects the government's temptation to print money when debt payment becomes very difficult or impaired. In this context, a relevant question is how long the risk-free rate could be "guaranteed" because printing money to pay debts simply devalues the risk-free rate by debasing the currency.

In the case of the Federal Reserve, it has "guaranteed" the fed funds rate to remain anchored at 0.25 percent for at least two years and thereby imposes a "risk-free" zone on the U.S. Treasury yield curve from bills at 0.01 percent to three-year Treasuries at 0.35 percent. Such a risk-free zone has been imposed by the Bank of Japan for the past 15 years, where Japanese T-bills up until 7-year maturity Japanese government bonds have risk-free returns ranging from 0.15 to 0.60 percent because those returns barely changed over. The Bank of England did the same by keeping its benchmark policy rate at 0.50 percent for the past three years. As a result one- to three-year U.K. government bond rates have been stuck at around 0.5 percent ever since the financial crisis. In Europe recently, German bills and two-year German government bonds reached 0.15 percent. Although the ECB has not implicitly or explicitly adopted a zero-bound policy, the rates on German bills and two-year maturity bonds show that the central bank may move at some point in that direction. Here is where the symptoms have overlap, whereas the risk-free zone on the yield curve constitutes a statutory rate cap. With average headline inflation running at around 2 to 3 percent in most major developed economies that have adopted the zero-bound policy, maintaining such a policy is a form of financial repression.

If central banks lock in their policy rates indefinitely, then forward short-term interest rates could present returns with lower realized volatility. And the longer the policy rate lock is guaranteed, the more interest-rate volatility concentrates at the longer end of the yield curve. This segment of the yield curve exhibits two types of risk premiums: (1) expectations of an interest-rate hike far out in the future and (2) uncertainty about deficit and debt sustainability. Market terminology calls this the *fiscal premium*, that is, the risk premium long-term interest rates reflect on the course of future fiscal policy. This is a change from before the crisis, when longer-term interest rates typically reflected the inflation risk premium.

The Japanese government bond market is a clear example. When the Bank of Japan (BoJ) reached near-zero bound in the late 1990s, it extended the zero-rate policy period from five years until the end 2006 and resumed it in 2008, a cumulative period of almost 15 years. The longer part (40 years) of the Japanese yield curve became the most volatile point. A measure is *historical basis point volatility*, which is calculated by multiplying the forward interest rate with the historical percentage price volatility. Earlier in the 2000s, 30- to 40-year Japanese government bond basis point volatility rose when the BoJ ran its zero interest-rate policy (ZIRP) from 2001 to 2006. Since 2011, 30-year U.S. Treasuries also have experienced an increase in basis point volatility after the Fed announced that it would keep the fed funds rate near zero for an extended period (conditionally), until at least the end of 2014. In contrast, there is Italy and Greece, where 30-year basis point volatility has fallen owing to a concentration of greater default risk at the front end of their respective yield curves when sovereign solvency risk rose sharply in the summer and fall of 2011. In the case of Italy and Greece, the notion of a risk-free rate made a complete turn-around as large government debt turned bad because the liabilities of the borrowers did not match the assets of the domestic lenders. As a result, Greek treasury bills were monopolized by Greek banks for liquidity collateral, which has capped their yields, so the treasury bills look to have a "guaranteed" return. The difference is that this is not a guarantee by the central bank but more a reflection of limited fiscal capacity on the part of the Greek government to fill the void in the ability to borrow by the financial sector. Thus there is a differentiation of the risk-free rate within global government bond markets. Markets with anchored central banks short rates that keep yield curves steep as a reflection of risk expressed by the increase in volatility premium in the longer end. Markets where governments are constrained because they inherited large debt in an economic downturn caused by limited capacity to expand fiscal policy see the short end of the yield curve bearing most of the risk. The more anchored the short end of the yield curve, the greater is the temptation to monetize. The more volatile the short end of the yield curve, the higher is the potential of a debt restructuring. These are symptoms of financial and sovereign debt crises.

To the point of increased volatility in longer-term rates, with a zero bound kept firmly in place, central bank policy rates look to have become statutory rate caps. With headline inflation still well above the policy rate, the rate cap set by central banks falls within Reinhart's definition of financial repression. There is another rate, however, one that has become perhaps an extension of the policy rate since 2009, namely, the *long-term real interest rate*. Academics have attempted to estimate a long-term "natural" real rate, whereas John Hicks researched in 1958 a 200-year history of yields on consols (a type of British government bond in which interest rates are paid on amounts without owing the principal) and found that interest rates stayed in the range of 3 to 3.5 percent. Recent researchers from the Bank of International Settlements (Amato, 2005) found for the United States and the United Kingdom an average long-term interest rate of 2.9 percent in real terms between 1965 and the present day.

It is noteworthy that the volatility of long-term rates has risen since 1999, seen from the increased standard deviations in Table 5.1.

Table 5.1   U.S. Term Premium in Longer-Term Interest Rates: Standard Deviations of Interest-Rate Changes*

	Fed Funds	3-Month T-Bill	10-Year Nominal Yield	10-Year Real Yield	Term Premium†	Term Premium Average
1965.1 to 1978.9	0.45	0.37	0.19	na	0.33	0.85
1986.1 to 1998.12	0.24	0.20	0.25	0.25	0.23	1.94
1999.1 to 2011.11	0.20	0.21	0.24	0.20	0.29	2.08

*Standard deviation of the first differences (i.e., $R_t - R_t - 1$) of the monthly averages of daily observations of interest rates measured in percentage points.
†10-year nominal yield *less* 3-month Treasury bill rate.

Moreover, the average *term premium* (defined as the difference between 10-year-maturity Treasury bonds and Treasury bills) rose to 208 basis points from 85 basis points from 1965 to 1978. To a degree, this also was caused by lower headline inflation, which was twice as low during 1999 and 2011 (average was 2.7 percent) than in previous decades (average 5.5 percent). Normally, under a higher-inflation scenario, you could expect the term premium to be larger because high inflation creates uncertainty.

In an era of lower inflation, though, this is reflected in a higher term premium that expresses uncertainty, specifically about the substitutability between short- and long-term rates. Remarkably, when there is perfect certainty about the future direction of short-term rates as central banks have put in place today, the maturity mix of debt would have no consequences because debt of different terms would be perfect substitutes for one another. The fact that the direction of debt-to-GDP ratios is all but uncertain has made debt maturities imperfect substitutes—hence the higher term premium not just in the United States but also in the United Kingdom, Japan, and Germany (average of 225 basis points measured by the slope between the 3-month bill and the 30-year bond yield). The rise in term premium also has been influenced by the pursuance of financial repression by certain countries' regulators (Basel III, a global financial framework for banks). Increased holdings of government bonds by banks and large investors made their behavior procyclic—a stronger appetite for safety during uncertain times, differentiation between the creditworthiness of countries. As the Euro debt crisis has shown, contagion effects attached when banks increased their holdings of bonds. Italy is a case where bank ownership of government debt accentuated interconnections between banks and sovereign risk. The differentiation within sovereign risk also drove large flows into safer, longer-dated bonds, where a shortage problem has risen; for example, foreign ownership of Australian bonds stands at a record high. Then there are the central banks that have purchased significant numbers of government bonds, absorbing most of the net issuance. The original idea came from Keynes, who said in 1936, "A remedy to slump is purchase of securities by the central bank until the long-term market rate is down to the limiting point." And then Bernanke pursued it according to his 2002 speech, although not yet as extremely. As he said then, "The Fed could enforce interest-rate ceilings by committing to make unlimited purchases."

Direct central bank involvement in the term structure of debt has an impact on debt management, whereas its demand creates supply. Influencing the long-term interest rate works as a countercyclic tool to entice capital formation, where with short rates at zero, monetary policy cannot be decided without knowledge of what the treasury intends to issue. The long-term rate therefore is a policy variable, whereby coordination between central bank and treasury plays a key role. The coordination, in turn, depends on whether a target range or quantity purchased is set to determine the long-term rate, which, in turn, can determine the change in maturity of the outstanding debt. Thus, with real 30-year rates near zero and the nominal rate being a policy variable and perhaps victim of safety flows at the same time, long-term rates may exhibit continuous term premium and volatility. Limited asset substitutability across the yield curve makes debt of different maturities imperfect substitutes, whereby a prolonged period of high government debt-to-GDP ratio adds to the uncertainty. This could imply that the long-term rate may stay mainly a policy variable—low in nominal terms, negative in real terms, but high in volatility.

Symptom Five: Short-Termism

Well-known concepts from finance are the *net present value* (NPV) and *internal rate of return* (IRR). The NPV is a summation of time series of cash flows discounted by the cost of capital (present values) minus the initial purchase price. A measure of the cost of capital can be the IRR, which is a discount rate that can determine whether an investment project would be desirable. A basic argument is that when the IRR is higher than a minimum required rate of return, the so-called hurdle rate, a project has a positive NPV and could be attractive. When the IRR is very high relative to the cost of capital, however, it is unrealistic to assume reinvestment at that high rate. This is especially damaging when comparing two investments with very different timings of cash flows. Hence the *hurdle rate* constitutes how rapidly the value of the dollar decreases in time and determines the payback period for the capital project when discounting forecast savings and spending back to present-day terms.

In a 2011 speech titled, "The Long Short," Bank of England's Haldane described *short-termism*, a form of investor myopia in which shorter-maturity cash flows are discounted at rates more appropriate for longer terms, yet the investment choices are returned to much shorter payback periods (stemming from CEO surveys). In other words, if the discount rate (IRR) is far higher than the hurdle rate as risk premiums are added, the difference between the average life of the investment and the expected payback term results in excessive discounting of cash flows. This leads to much lower future present values than otherwise would have been the case. Haldane sees short-termism sharply on the rise as equity risk premiums have risen (he estimates an average risk premium of 5.9 percent) with more discounting (5 to 10 percent) lengthening payback periods (average 9 years from 3 to 5 years), leading to too low investment in longer-duration projects.

A prerequisite to short-termism is what was described earlier by Ray Dalio of Bridgewater as the discounted value of expectations of future earnings. When such expectations are high, they encourage borrowing and thereby consumption of future earnings today. When debt levels get excessive, a present-value effect occurs when the discount rate is slashed, it drives asset prices higher and entices even more borrowing. When discount rates can't be lowered further, this may lead to a downward spiral of asset liquidations. Thus, as discount rates have fallen since 2008 as central banks eased interest rates, this has led to higher risk premiums being added to future cash flows of bonds and stocks, yielding current present values that are unnaturally above future present values. Since the present-value effect is no longer there, Carmen Reinhart identified a new kind of financial repression by nonmarket forces (central banks) through methods such as QE. QE's effect led to negative real rates, adding more risk premium into forward rates historically well above where discount rates (spot nominal yields) currently are. There is short-termism in government bonds as nominal yields are repressed by the central bank shortening the payback period to facilitate large redemptions. At the same time, the actual payback period is far longer because markets have identified debt sustainability risks across sovereigns. This has led to excessive discounting of cash flows in, for example, Greece, Portugal, and Ireland but not yet in the United States or the United Kingdom because those markets experience central bank–induced financial repression. This repression started before the crisis as market confidence allowed the U.S. and U.K. governments to borrow from future earnings at lower nominal rates that were lowered further by aggressive monetary easing in and after the crisis. Hence the *sovereign hurdle rate* (nominal bond yields) has fallen far below the IRR, represented by yields expressed in forward markets. The sovereign hurdle rate determines the actual versus expected payback period and thus the appropriate level of NPV of government bonds. Because the hurdle rate is influenced, an unusually high risk premium could lead eventually to excessive discounting owing to short-termism.

Symptom Six: An Interlude of Crises

Reinhart and Rogoff's empirical work has another important conclusion, namely, evidence of a sequence in crises. Whenever a financial crisis occurs, it tends to be followed by a sovereign crisis that ends in an inflation crisis. The sequence is related to monetary policy before the financial crisis and during and after the sovereign crisis. Reinhart and Rogoff show in their semiannual work, *This Time It's Different*, that there is a historical relationship between inflation and external default. As demonstrated in Figure 5.8, Reinhart and Rogoff use an empirical data set that stretches from 1900 until 2006 that shows strong correlation between the share of countries in default on debt and the number of countries experiencing high inflation (defined by Reinhart and Rogoff as inflation over 20 percent per annum).

Underlying the default and inflation trend are *asset bubbles*, as depicted in Figure 5.9. This chart takes the asset bubbles that happened in the United States from stocks, to housing, to bonds, to commodities. Driven by significantly easy monetary policy that brings down funding rates such as the London Interbank Offered Rate (LIBOR),

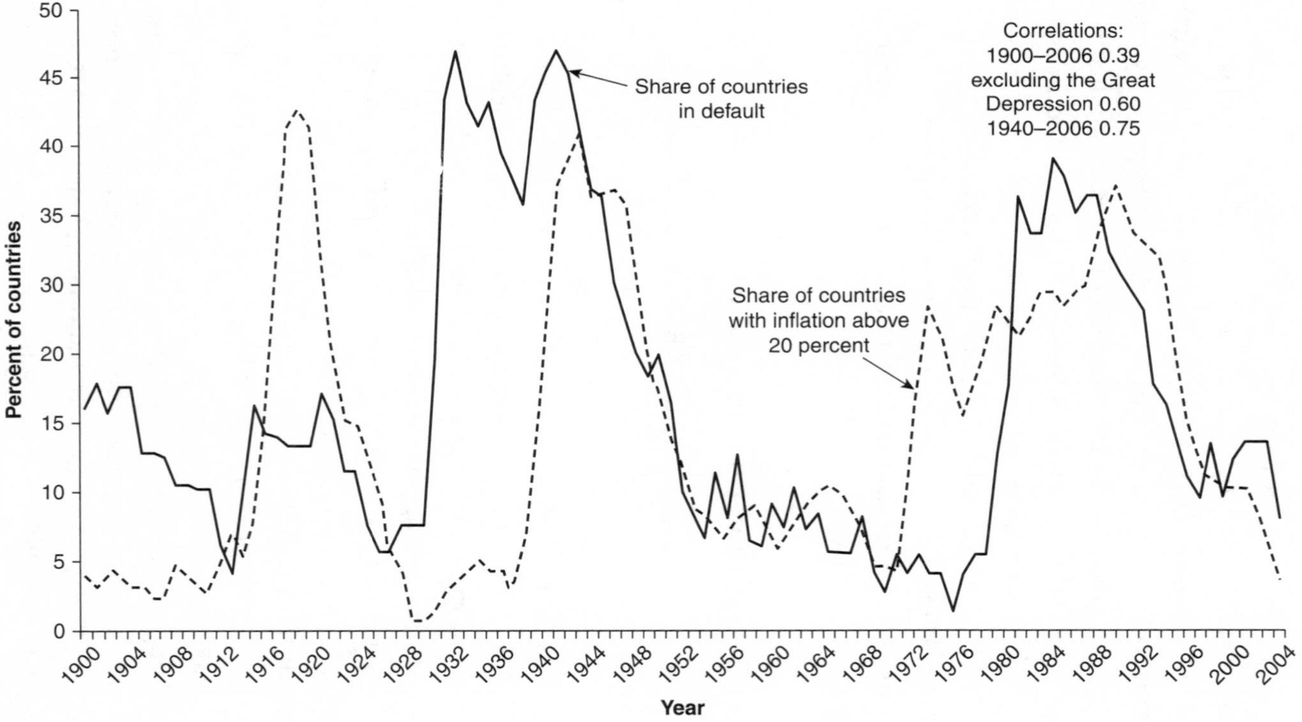
Percent of countries
0
5
10
15
20
25
30
35
40
45
50
1900
1904
1908
1912
1916
1920
1924
1928
1932
1936
1940
1944
1948
1952
1956
1960
1964
1968
1972
1976
1980
1984
1988
1992
1996
2000
2004
Year
Share of countries in default
Share of countries with inflation above 20 percent
Correlations:
1900–2006 0.39
excluding the Great Depression 0.60
1940–2006 0.75

Figure 5.8 Default and inflation: inflation and external default, 1900–2006.

(*Source:* Reinhart and Rogoff., 2008)

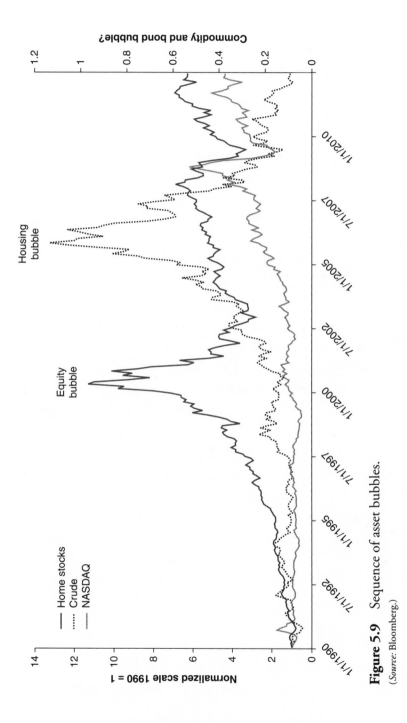

Figure 5.9 Sequence of asset bubbles.

(*Source:* Bloomberg.)

125

asset bubbles are fed when recessions occur. When default and inflation come down, consistently low LIBORs can set up new assets bubbles, such as, for example, today in gold, crude oil, U.S. Treasuries, and technology stocks.

What's more, historical default rates shared among major developed countries are currently still very low. Even after the financial crisis, the economy struggles with a liquidity trap, and there is evidence of financial repression; markets express different outcomes that make the likelihood of inflation *and* default occurring at the same time much greater. How great depends on the speed of debt deleveraging of different balance sheets, the willingness of monetary policy makers to go to extremes, and the economy as a whole experiencing continuous underutilization of production and structural unemployment. As insurance against default, the credit default swaps (CDS) market reflected more bimodal outcomes. This led to two market phenomena: (1) The weighted-average corporate CDS risk premium fell below that of the weighted-average sovereign CDS risk premium, and (2) emerging-market sovereign CDS risk premium came in close proximity of the developed-market sovereign CDS. This combination of dislocation in premiums implies a transfer of balance sheets as crises go from one to another. The fact is that corporate and some sovereign emerging-market balance sheets are healthy; that is, they exhibit low levels of debt and stronger capital and liquidity positions and in general receive confidence from financial markets. When asset bubbles develop and the stage of Mynski's Ponzi finance is reached, a balance sheet crisis may occur that has to be cushioned by another balance sheet. The sequence of balance sheets goes with expansion of one to (over) compensate for the contraction as a result of a "glut" that may cause another glut.

A general glut is seen when supply exceeds demand, specifically when there is excess production across all fields of production that cannot be consumed adequately. This can lead to sharp price falls when such excess is accompanied by underproduction in other parts of the economy. Jean Baptiste Say was one of the first economists who argued in the 1800s that although there may be gluts in several markets, they can be balanced by shortages in others. Say derived his concept from *laissez-faire:* A supply imbalance is a transient and linear phenomenon that is corrected by an adjustment in demand. This is in contrast to the general glut view, which sees supply imbalance as a nonlinear phenomenon that can be adjusted only via sharp price adjustments. Another economist, Adam Smith, who lived around the same time as Say, was an advocate of the glut view. Adam Smith brought forward his well-known "invisible hand" idea, which was one of a self-regulated market that creates its own balance by price adjustment. As discussed in the introduction to this chapter, such economic ideas were on the shelf, not in direct focus by financial markets. This changed when the aftermath of the financial crisis sought answers to how such a crisis happened. A glut was viewed as one of the causes, a savings glut described by Bernanke in his speech, "The Global Savings Glut and the U.S. Current Account Deficit" in 2005 as "high desired saving and the low prospective returns to domestic investment, the mature industrial economies as a group seek to run current account surpluses and thus to lend abroad." This has led to lower interest rates and has helped to create credit. But it also created a glut sequence in financial debt issuance. Figure 5.10 depicts the sequence: First, there is an initial glut, where, for example, securitized mortgage and credit products swelled to a peak of 1.5 trillion dollars in 2007. As demand started to wane for these products, the glut view came to life as securitized mortgage and credit markets corrected to be lower in price. As a result, issuance in that sector fell sharply by 2008 and turned into a shortage. But less credit creation had an adverse effect on the economy, and via automatic stabilizers in government spending that kick in when a recession starts, another glut appeared in global sovereign bond issuance that went from $750 billion before the crisis to $3 trillion by

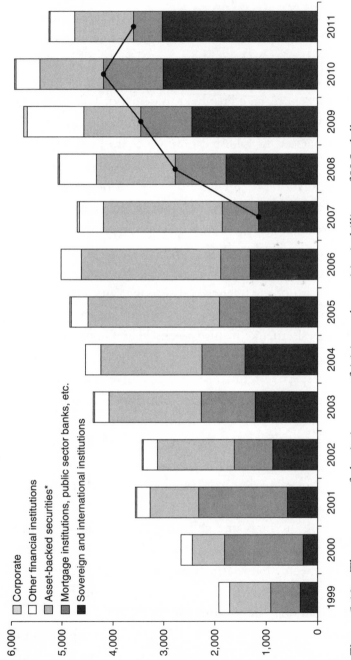

Figure 5.10   The sequence of glut in issuance of AAA-rated securities in billions of U.S. dollars.

Note: For 2011, full-year estimate based on January to October data.

*ABS, MBS, and covered bonds.

(*Source:* Bank of International Settlements.)

2011, as shown in Figure 5.10. As additional stimulus in the form of QE was layered onto the economy, the portfolio balance effect enticed private-sector money into risk assets, and the same effect induced new supply creation in markets such as investment-grade corporate bonds, high-yield bonds, and emerging-market bonds. Figure 5.10 shows this too, where the debt issuance of corporate and other financial institutions rose since 2009.

This is a *layered* domino effect. A savings glut in 2005 led to trade imbalances that eventually led to unwinding through an adjustment of a glut in the credit markets. Policy makers responded with a stimulus to entice credit creation that resulted into debt gluts absorbed by institutions driven by financial repression–type regulation. The amounts of debt sitting on those balance sheets against a glut of issuance in that specific debt will at some point be questioned in terms of solvency and liquidity. As the glut sees a price correction, more policy stimulus will restart another glut of debt. This debt creation also plays into asset bubbles following each other in a similar sequence as the NPV effect of asset prices–induced debt creation gets driven higher until no longer viewed as rational. When the general glut view holds, then one could expect further price corrections in any of the asset markets to correct the overall supply imbalance. This can bring along an interlude of crisis, whereas so far the 2008 financial crisis went into a sovereign crisis in Europe that caused a banking crisis there as well. What Figure 5.10 also shows is that a debt maturity period evolved between 2007 and 2011, where a glut of government bonds needs to be rebalanced simultaneously with increasing financial debt rollover. But there is no future shortage to offset gluts. This phenomenon is most prevalent in Europe, and the next two chapters describe in detail the root causes of the crisis and how this can be viewed from a financial domino effect framework.

Part 2

Application of the Financial Domino Effects Framework

Chapter 6

Disintegration of the European Monetary Union: A Prelude

In this chapter, the financial domino effect framework that was discussed in preceding chapters will be applied to a real-time crisis, namely, the European sovereign debt crisis. To better understand the root causes of this crisis, this chapter focuses mainly on the description of a number of factors that have contributed to today's turmoil. These factors were part of a lengthy buildup process before the first effects were seen. Like an earthquake that is long overdue, warned about for years, the initial tremors of this crisis served as warning signals but were followed by a big bang that was unexpected. Such was the case for the sovereign debt crisis in Europe, where after years of perceived safety, government bond markets suddenly experienced wild swings and volatility. The crisis has become so severe that a credit crunch and deep recession may even lead to the Armageddon scenario of a breakup of the European Monetary Union (EMU).

The buildup to the present crisis solidified as a result of three factors that continue to play a significant role:

1. The foundation of the EMU during the blueprint phase of 1989–1991 and subsequent early violation of fiscal deficit and debt rules
2. Europe's first crisis, the currency crisis within the exchange-rate mechanism
3. Imbalances via labor markets, current accounts, and effective exchange rates

The foundation of the EMU looked to be sound in 1991, when the Treaty of Maastricht was signed, but the first weaknesses appeared during Europe's first crisis, which later led to an implosion of the European Exchange Rate Mechanism (ERM). After the ERM crisis ended in the fall of 1993, currencies from Italy, Spain, Portugal, and France were devalued, and the economies of those countries were able to recover. Since the European economic cycle turned favorably—helped by a strong U.S. economy—transition to the EMU received strong political support. The transition process to become a full monetary union was to be achieved through several phases, as outlined in the 1989 Delors Report.

Transition to a Monetary Union

The Delors Committee during 1985–1988 developed a blueprint for a transition to a monetary union in Europe. The Delors Report set out a three-stage monetary integration process with a strategy of gradualism. The process was to increase the degree of convergence and cooperation during each phase so as to have a smooth introduction of monetary unification in the final stage. The stages were first to abolish capital controls and strengthen the degree of cooperation among the European central banks. In the second stage, a new institution, the European Monetary Institute (EMI), was to function as a precursor for the European Central Bank (ECB) until it became operational in the final stage, when exchange rates were irrevocably fixed, the euro was created, and monetary unification was achieved. The transition for each country to the monetary union was made conditional on the basis of *convergence criteria*. The criteria were formalized in the Maastricht Treaty in 1991, which embodied two principles: (1) The transition to monetary union was to be gradual, and (2) not all European Union (EU) countries had to join the monetary union at the same time.

The implications of gradualism were seen at the time as self-defeating because gradualism carried the risk of failure to full convergence and could work as a destabilizing force, especially when countries complied with the strict budget norms during a recession. This occurred when the recession of the early 1990s created a lack of commitment on the part of future EMU members, and the result was that only Luxembourg and Ireland satisfied all the convergence criteria. Moreover, meeting the criteria became a further challenge in the mid-1990s when debate suggested that the EMU might start as a tier 1 and tier 2 process involving "ins" and "outs"—that is, core countries such as Germany, the Benelux, and France would form the EMU first tier, followed by the Mediterranean countries as tier 2 at a later stage. The Venn diagram created by UBS Research in Figure 6.1 explains the "ins"—countries that can match the Maastricht criteria, countries whose political system has a willingness to do so, and countries whose economies make them an optimal currency area—and the "not ins" (i.e., "outs").

The differentiation between ins and outs was one of the reasons for the call for a gradual transition to monetary unification, considering the sheer size differences between countries. Another reason was that the convergence criteria were formulated in such a way as to make

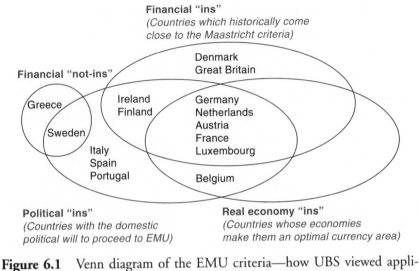

Figure 6.1   Venn diagram of the EMU criteria—how UBS viewed applicants in 1996.
(*Source:* UBS Research.)

it unlikely that all 12 European countries would be able to satisfy the criteria at the same time. Other arguments had been brought forward by academia, but it was in Germany's interest to keep the monetary union relatively small, so German authorities insisted that countries must satisfy the criteria before they would be able to be part of the monetary union.

The philosophy of gradualism was challenged at the time by several opinions on achieving monetary transition. For example, the transition could be achieved through so-called shock therapy. In this case, direct monetary reform was seen as advantageous by creating one hard currency on day one of the monetary union. The strength of such a currency then would allow quicker convergence of inflation expectations between countries. Another view was expressed as the *theory of optimum currency areas*, which argued that a monetary union could be established if such factors as wages, labor, and capital could endure with high flexibility and mobility. And then there was the idea of a parallel-currency approach by introducing a hard ECU monetary unit that would drive national currencies out and create convergence through the economic process.

In the development of the Maastricht criteria, optimal currency area theory and the idea of a parallel currency did not play a role. Monetary integration progressed slowly in the 1990s, and eventually all countries technically met the Maastricht criteria. This was solidified in 1997, when member states adopted the Growth and Stability Pact (SGP) as a fiscal disciplinary and enforcement mechanism in the future EMU. The actual criteria that member states were required to respect consisted of an annual budget deficit of no more than 3 percent of gross domestic product (GDP) and a national debt that is lower than 60 percent of GDP. The SGP was proposed initially by German Finance Minister Theo Waigel. Because Germany had long maintained a low-inflation policy, the German government hoped to ensure continuation of that policy through the SGP. The idea was not just to limit the ability of governments to exert inflationary pressures on the European economy but also not to relax under lower interest rates because their monetary policies were connected to the Bundesbank anti-inflation record. Two years prior to entering the EMU, most countries, with the exception of Ireland, Luxembourg, and Finland, did not meet the maximum 3 percent deficit convergence criterion. Similarly, in terms of the debt as a percentage of GDP criterion, most countries barely stayed under the hurdle of 60 percent, and Belgium, Italy, and Greece were the outliers from the start, running debt-to-GDP ratios in excess of 120 percent. So the SGP's institutional foundation had been weakened from the outset by spending and taxation policies that remained the responsibility of national governments and parliaments. There is a vested democratic legitimacy to the idea that European national parliaments must address spending and taxation decisions. As in any democracy, decisions undergo an elaborate process, and in Europe that process is embedded in the national European political spectrum. The basis for this argument is that deficit procedures have political legitimacy only if they are determined by national governments that face the threat of being punished by their home voter base in the wake of severe austerity measures. In contrast, the European Commission (EC) does not face the prospect of being punished by voters, and therefore, the EC lacks a level of democratic legitimacy because there is no mechanism to make the EC accountable before an electorate for its actions. This was always seen as a key weakness of the EMU. Without having a centralized government that would have governance powers to severally and jointly guarantee government liabilities, many economists saw the EMU as doomed.

Because there were great differences between the deficits and debts of the various countries, naturally this would determine the interest differentials in government bonds. In fact, such differentials were driven more by political uncertainty on the one hand and rising inflation on the other. When by 1996 a new exchange-rate mechanism (ERM II) was agreed on with wider bands, it allowed greater flexibility for European central banks to increase short-term interest rates to lower inflation in line with the Maastricht criteria. This essentially set the stage for a convergence of the long-term interest rates of such countries as Italy, Spain, and others relative to Germany. As central banks in Italy and Spain became bolder in fighting inflation by hiking interest rates, interest-rate differentials initially became wider. Once the political situation in Italy stabilized and inflation started to fall, a bail-in effect occurred, and Long Term Capital Management (LTCM) built a significant position in Italian bonds, betting on the convergence trade.

As shown in Figure 6.2, yield spreads between Italy, Spain, and Portugal narrowed to that of Germany from 1996 onward. This convergence helped to set the stage for entry to the EMU because falling inflation rates and convergence trades masked the need to achieve deficit and debt criteria. Without a proper central governmental mechanism and with deficit and debt levels already above intended thresholds, the interest-rate convergence that started in 1996 was a conundrum. In addition, the Asian financial crisis in 1997 and the

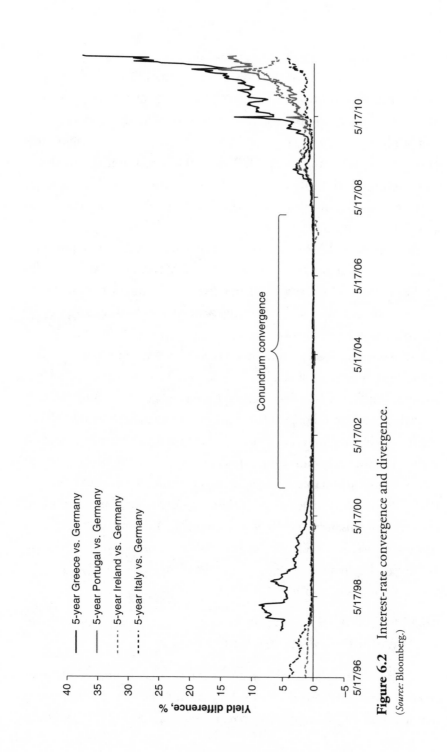

Figure 6.2 Interest-rate convergence and divergence.

(*Source:* Bloomberg.)

LTCM implosion in 1998 did not stop the rate convergence. The fact that adoption of the euro would put into circulation a currency with a strong anti-inflation bias and a Bundesbank-like monetary policy was an anchor most of the Mediterranean countries never really achieved. As a result, the convergence of spreads led to an undershooting of fundamentals between the years 2000 and 2008 because investors didn't fully appreciate the different risks between countries. Therefore, as Figure 6.2 shows, investors became much more perceptive, leading to significant divergence.

A number of EMU collapse scenarios are possible, but the cost-benefit analysis of any country leaving the EMU must address a trade-off: Bond yields would soar further, currencies would be devalued, and payment systems would be severely damaged, offsetting any potential competitive gains to be made. The possibility of forming a new but smaller monetary union has received attention in the media. Specifically, now bond yields in countries such as Greece, Ireland, Portugal, and even Italy have reached levels where debt can rise exponentially. Without the possibility of an independent lender of last resort printing unlimited currency or successfully implementing labor market reforms to regain competitiveness, restructuring of government debt becomes inevitable. Such was the case during the ERM crisis in 1992–1993, when it became clear that the system could not bear monetary policy misaligned with fundamentals. A round of speculative attacks occurred, leading up to devaluations and eventual implosion of the ERM system.

ERM Crisis of 1992–1993:
The Incomplete Monetary Union

A monetary arrangement between countries that is not a full monetary union but follows a set of rules that link their monetary policies is known as an *incomplete monetary union*. Prior to the EMU, an example was the European Exchange Rate Mechanism (ERM). The system had an adjustable peg nature that defined bands in which bilateral exchange rates of member countries could fluctuate. The member countries would adjust their monetary policies to maintain their currencies within in a fluctuation band but without subordinating to a central monetary policy. The bands of fluctuation were characterized by a set of adjustable bilateral central parities and margins that defined the bandwidth of permissible fluctuation (±2.25 percent and ±6 percent for the Italian lira). There also was creation of the precursor to the euro currency, namely, an artificial unit of account named the *European currency unit* (ECU). The ECU was only a unit of account and not a medium of exchange, and no ECU notes or coins were issued and used to conduct transactions. It was merely an accounting unit constructed as a fixed basket of European currencies. The ECU was a dummy common exchange rate against which other currencies fluctuated within their bands and central parities.

When in 1992 economic fundamentals deteriorated, foreign-exchange (FX) markets became wary that the ERM bandwidths were relatively too tight for what the fundamentals were suggesting. In other words, the central banks had a commitment to maintain their currency band, but the FX market recognized that this was nonbinding. That is, although there was an agreement and enhanced cooperation among central banks that linked their monetary policies, an individual central bank could at any time devalue its currency. To have this option against a backdrop of deteriorating economies made tight monetary policy misaligned. This created an incentive for speculators to bet on devaluations. The ERM crisis is an example of an academic idea called an $n - 1$ *problem:* Within a system of fixed exchange rates, there is only $n - 1$ exchange rate with $n - 1$ monetary authority. The other monetary authorities are forced to adjust their policy to maintain a fixed exchange rate, with only one monetary authority that is free to set policy independently.

The system therefore has one degree of freedom, where there is either an asymmetric solution (one country takes leadership, and others follow) or a symmetric solution (full cooperation among countries within a system of [sterilized] interventions). The ERM crisis suffered from asymmetry in that Germany could freely set (and significantly tightened) monetary policy, whereas other countries were forced to adjust monetary policy to maintain a fixed exchange rate versus the deutschmark. Another striking feature of the ERM crisis was the debate about currency realignment. In 1992, there was a huge division among European officials that colored the discussion. Germany was keen on generalized currency realignment, but no other country (except Italy) was willing to discuss it. The pressure was put on the Bundesbank to cut rates, which it refused to do, and when currency pressures mounted, the realization set in that there were limits to reserves to defend currencies. The Bundesbank defended the Italian lira but decided not to extend unlimited deutschmarks out of fear ofr inflation. The 1992 ERM crisis was the result of speculative attacks not just against the Italian lira but also against the French franc based on testing France's commitment to maintaining a parity rate and adjusting monetary policy accordingly. The ERM crisis is known for its contagion effects accentuated by speculators—the "shorts." A short speculator typically will trade in a brief time window, and this intensifies speculative attacks. The ERM crisis was essentially a speculative attack on central banks' reserves that within a short period of time exhausted them and therefore led to a collapse of the system.

The collapse of ERM also was characterized by specific cases such as the Italian lira, but it also involved the British pound, the Danish referendum of 1992, and Swedish krona—until the crisis ended with the French franc. When in September 1992 a gentlemen's agreement was reached for a general realignment involving a 3.5 percent devaluation of the lira combined with an interest-rate cut by Germany, the result was a disaster. The first ERM realignment in many years made the market aware that after much political horse trading, devaluation was possible. Since only the Italian lira was devalued and this wasn't followed by realignments by other countries (yet they could do so at any moment), market speculation grew quickly. This was fueled by Bundesbank President Schlesinger, who strongly hinted at more devaluation rounds. A specific focus became the French franc. As part of the core currency link under the ERM, France and Germany would do what they could to defend the franc. As the franc came under speculative attack, the central banks of France and Germany intervened aggressively to hold their exchange-rate link by buying francs and selling marks. The countries succeeded, but it was only momentarily—it was more like a delay of the inevitable.

The Bank of France defended its currency, but nearly depleted its foreign-currency reserves. Speculative attacks continued to hit the franc because speculators knew that France needed lower interest rates to help stimulate the economy and reduce unemployment. The Bank of France raised interest rates to defend the franc, and both the central banks of both France and Germany continued to intervene directly to support the franc. The rise in French interest rates continued to hurt the French economy. And since German interest rates were too high, only a cut in German rates would be able to save the franc. Continued speculative attacks against the franc proved to be impossible to beat, so Germany and France gave up defending the exchange-rate link. The EU finance ministers and central bankers decided to allow the currency trading bands to fluctuate within 15 percent around a central rate on August 2, 1993. Once again, the speculators won and locked in their profits by buying back the devalued franc. The German central bank tried to prop up the French franc, but it didn't succeed because it was not seen as an unlimited intervention.

Another specific case involved the British pound, which after several years of shadowing the deutschmark, entered the ERM in a band ±6 percent. Since inflation and interest rates were running over

15 percent, the United Kingdom also was hurt by the rapid depreciation of the U.S. dollar, a currency in which many British export goods were priced. Britain's prime minister and cabinet members tried vehemently to prop up a sinking pound, and withdrawal from the monetary system the country had joined two years prior was in their view the last resort. The Bank of England raised interest rates to 10 percent and authorized the spending of billions of pounds to buy up the sterling being frantically sold on the currency markets, but the measures failed to prevent the pound from falling lower than its minimum level in the ERM. The British Treasury took the decision to defend sterling's position, believing that to devalue would be to promote inflation. On September 16, 1992, the British government announced a rise in the base interest rate from an already high 10 percent to 12 percent to tempt speculators to buy pounds. Despite this and a promise later the same day to raise base rates again to 15 percent, dealers kept selling pounds, convinced that the government would not stick to its promise. An emergency meeting on September 16, 1992, between then Chancellor Lamont, Prime Minister Major, and Foreign Secretary Hurd produced an agreement to withdraw the pound from the ERM. That day became known as "Black Wednesday" because that also was the day marking the end of the lira in the ERM. Black Wednesday was followed by speculative attacks against the Portuguese escudo, Spanish peseta, Irish punt, and even the Greek drachma (Figure 6.3). Evidently, the FX market sought out countries with deteriorated fundamentals once the weakness of the ERM system was fully exposed.

The situation intensified when Denmark held a public referendum on the Maastricht Treaty on June 2, 1992, and Danish voters rejected ratification of the treaty. The referendum outcome was seen as a blow to the European integration progress. Along with a small majority in French and Irish referenda, it gave the international community the impression of a slim consensus backing European integration. Adding fuel to speculative fires enflaming the ERM system, the Danish

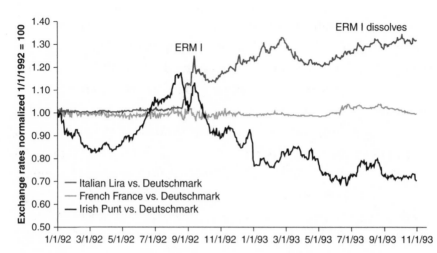

Figure 6.3 Currencies during the ERM crisis of 1992–1993.
(*Source:* Bloomberg.)

government negotiated in the Edinburgh Agreement an *opt-out clause*, where Denmark would not be obliged to switch from its Danish krona to the euro. This example was followed by Sweden and the United Kingdom, which also negotiated opt-out clauses. Distinctively, both the United Kingdom and Sweden, like Denmark, also tied adoption of the euro to a public referendum. By 2003, Sweden held a referendum on the euro, and the United Kingdom held an economic test based on five criteria before euro adoption would move to a referendum. In both cases, adoption of the euro was rejected. In the end, the ERM system could not be held together, and countries abandoned their currency bands and currencies became free floating.

Imbalances Before the EMU and Today

A currency union by its nature should have some "imbalances" through trading partners. One major imbalance in the EMU lies elsewhere, namely, in the area of labor markets. Since transition to the monetary union received more momentum, the "rigidity" in labor markets across Europe remained. Labor market rigidity can be described as the total change in real wages as a percentage of total wages. ECB studies (see the 2006 paper titled, "How Wages Change: Micro Evidence from the International Wage Flexibility Project," for example) have shown that U.S. wage rigidity declined during the 1980s and 1990s as pattern bargaining among labor unions diminished. Euro-zone unions, on the other hand, remained very strong in collective wage bargaining. The 2006 paper shows that average real wage rigidity, defined as wage freezes or wage cuts as a fraction of total workers in the labor force, is very low for the United States at 10 percent but much higher for the Euro zone at an average of 25 percent. The density of labor unions, when measured as a percentage of workers who are members of a labor union, remains low for the United States at 20 percent versus an average for the Euro zone of 45 percent. When plotting wage rigidity against labor union density, as shown in Figure 6.4, it is clear that the United States is the least rigid in wages, whereas the Euro zone experiences far greater rigidity. In optimal currency area terms, the United States seems to have greater labor factor flexibility. This labor market imbalance is a major contributing factor to why certain countries lost competitiveness. In the absence of currency devaluation, fiscal austerity has to be accompanied by labor wage adjustment to maintain a growth level that doesn't cause government insolvency. As Figure 6.4 shows, highest rigidity occurs in countries such as Italy and Greece, as well as France, that have high government debt and deficits and as a result now pay much higher government rates than their nominal GDP growth. Finland is an exception owing to extremely small deficit and government debt, whereas Sweden has its own currency.

The other imbalances are the twin deficits described in Chapter 2 as an economic domino effect. The imbalance was already large before the crisis, but it grew even further after the financial crisis. Figure 6.5 shows that the same group of countries as in Figure 6.4 that experience

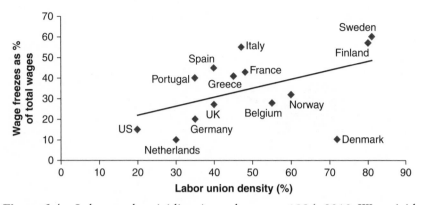

Figure 6.4   Labor market rigidity: Annual average, 1994–2010. Wage rigidity is total wage freezes as a percentage of total wages. Labor union density is the percentage of workers who are members of a labor union.
(*Source:* OECD.)

labor rigidity also suffer from the twin deficits. Unwind of these deficits in a fixed exchange-rate mechanism has caused a spike in real interest rates in those countries that have contracted credit to households and businesses. As the twin-deficit hypothesis goes, when an economy is borrowing from foreigners to finance both deficits and domestic savings remains the same, a sudden currency depreciation or a rise in domestic interest rates can occur. The higher real rates do not attract sufficient capital to offset both deficits, and without a means to devalue the currency, the twin-deficits problem is another element of asymmetry that the EMU suffers. The asymmetry lies in the concept of optimal currency areas. According to Robert A. Mundell, founder of the theory on optimal currency areas, there are two ways the pace of employment within countries with a current account deficit is set: In currency areas made up of different countries with different national currencies, the pace of employment within deficit countries is set by the willingness of the surplus countries to generate inflation. However, in a currency area consisting of many regions and a single currency, the pace of inflation is set by the willingness of central monetary authorities to allow

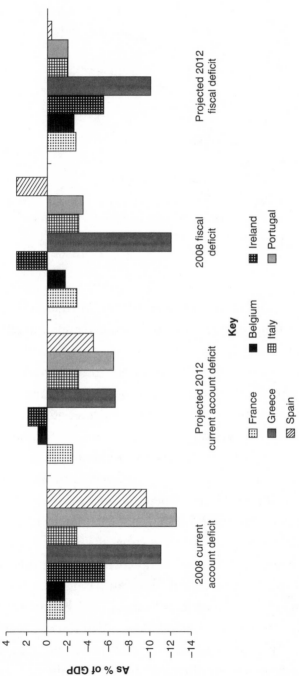

Figure 6.5 Twin deficits: 2008 versus 2012.

(*Source:* IMF, World Economic Outlook, October 2011.)

unemployment in the deficit regions. To combine both currency areas into an "optimal" one, there has to be coordination among central banks to avoid unemployment and inflation, whereby surplus countries help to adjust deficit countries. Applied to Figure 6.5, this is the issue in the EMU today: Under a system of seventeen central banks that are coordinated but have no autonomy, there is no automatic adjustment mechanism. Thus the twin-deficit problem continues to be in play.

The Euro Debt Crisis: 2009–Present

What is commonly known is that the *Euro-zone debt crisis* began in the fall of 2009 when the newly elected Greek government under Papandreou discovered a large gap in its budget. However, the crisis actually started sooner, namely, shortly after the Lehman Brothers event in 2008, when spreads on Austrian government bonds widened as a result of its domestic bank's loan exposure to Eastern Europe. Economist Paul Krugman first voiced his concern by writing in his *New York Times* blog in April 2009: "Austria's lending in the region 'is off the charts' compared with anyone else's, and that means some serious risk given that emerging Europe is experiencing the mother of all currency crises."

Already then there was acknowledgment that indirect externalities of bank lending tied to countries with current-account deficits could be transmitted back into contaminating the sovereign. Much earlier, in 2006, Professor Roubini predicted that Italy and potentially a group of other countries such as Portugal, Spain, and Greece might have to exit the EMU if "serious economic reforms" were not implemented rapidly. Roubini said in a speech in 2006:

> It is not a foregone conclusion, but if Italy does not reform, an exit from the EMU within five years is not totally unlikely. Indeed, like Argentina, Italy faces a growing competitiveness loss given an increasingly overvalued currency and the risk of falling exports and growing

current-account deficit. The growth slowdown will make the public deficit and debt worse and potentially unsustainable over time. And if devaluation cannot be used to reduce real wages, the real exchange rate overvaluation will be undone via a slow and painful process of wage and price deflation.

In the first weeks of 2010, there was renewed anxiety about excessive national debt. Frightened investors demanded higher interest rates from several governments with higher debt levels or deficits. This, in turn, made it difficult for governments to finance further budget deficits and service existing high debt levels. Elected officials focused on austerity measures (e.g., higher taxes and lower expenses), contributing to social unrest and significant debate among economists, many of whom advocate greater deficits when economies are struggling. Especially in countries where government budget deficits and sovereign debts have increased sharply, a *crisis of confidence* has emerged with the widening of bond yield spreads and risk insurance on credit default swap (CDS) contracts. This crisis of confidence is a self-fulfilling prophecy. Thus the financial domino effect framework introduced in Chapter 1 can be applied directly to an analysis of the Euro-zone debt crisis to provide a sense of how to navigate such a crisis in the future. Although the EMU is unique among past currency unions that at some point came under the threat of dissolution, the nature of the Lisbon and Maastricht treaties, the ECB, and the measures taken to stem the crisis all have elements of the financial domino effect framework. The ERM crisis of 1992–1993 had a similar kind of domino effect style, and hence a comparison along the framework is relevant.

Chapter 7

The Euro-Zone Debt Crisis in the Context of the Financial Domino Effects Framework

The events during the European Exchange Rate Mechanism (ERM) crisis followed each other at a rapid pace analogous to a snowball effect; that is, the ERM crisis had many elements of domino effects. The speculative nature of the crisis was viewed as an underlying force steering those effects. In reality, the speculative forces were a reflection of a strong connection between asset prices, economic fundamentals, and political and monetary leadership. The nature of the ERM crisis had a sequence that reveals strong parallels between the ERM and the recent debt crisis in Europe.

Two basic principles are the fundamental drivers of each crisis:

1. Monetary/fiscal policy rules set by one country that force other countries to adjust policy that becomes misaligned with fundamentals. This causes asymmetry within the system and exposes its weaknesses. Despite rules and agreements, there is no

binding agreement that prevents a country from abandoning the system.

2. Presence of balance sheets that are constrained by rules or policy to stem speculative contagion.

These two principles create a virtual loop—a sequence of events that caused the crisis to repeat itself from country to country. This loop became self-defeating, through a circle of negative feedback from market participants and policy makers. But the causes of the domino effects were unique to the debt crisis. The Euro-zone debt crisis could be called a *crisis of confidence in public debt*. The confidence loss, however, had a self-fulfilling character, and there were several factors that played a role. For one, the European leadership became increasingly challenged as the crisis intensified. A string of cacophony, disagreements, and divisions that colored discussions among political leaders culminated in crisis summits that presented climax moments the markets quickly judged as agreements without foundation. These factors helped to further erode the confidence of longer-term investors, rating agencies, and even the European Central Bank (ECB). Combined elements of the negative feedback loop present a sequence, and they rank in the following order:

1. The option to abandon the system of rules and agreements
2. The games of chicken among a multitude of players
3. The asymmetry of the system
4. The presence of limited resources
5. Separation
6. A unique case
7. Embedded subordination and two-tiered markets
8. Soft restructuring
9. The role of rating agencies
10. The lender of last resort

11. "Trilemma"
12. The economic and political breakup of the European Monetary
    Union (EMU)

This ranking reveals a self-defeating cycle—a chain of events that functions like dominoes affecting one another. The following sections will explain why.

The Option to Abandon

Markets tend to recognize early when policy is misaligned with fundamentals. This can fuel speculative behavior and expectations of a breakdown in the sustainability of the system. Although monetary policy was seen as too tight during the ERM crisis, European fiscal policy today is viewed as being too tight against a backdrop of sharply weakening economies. Since policy making is based on a set of rules that link policy, comparison between the ERM episode and today's crisis centers on the weakness of that linkage. Central banks ran a centralized policy to maintain currency bands within the ERM. The European governments formed a fiscal compact to run a central fiscal policy based on rules and debt brakes. In both cases, the agreements were nonbinding because no country "fully" subordinated its sovereignty. The option exists to abandon the agreements at any time. The market recognizes this option as a weakness and exploits it with either speculation or liquidation via an "escape valve" that can compound the effects of the feedback loop. During the European debt crisis, when bond yields surged as investor confidence waned when austerity measures were announced, this adversely affected economies by tightening credit conditions. A weaker economy can suffer worse debt and deficit projections, which, in turn, can lead to expectations of rating downgrades in combination with rising bond yields, which indeed happen like a self-fulfilling prophecy.

Policy makers react with more austerity measures, but given a lack of credibility, such measures fail to regain investor confidence. The feedback loop is similar to that in the ERM crisis, where investors sold currencies as they lost confidence in the ability of central banks to maintain currencies within their predetermined bands. As currencies weakened, central banks had to respond with tighter monetary policy to keep the currency in the band. And the tighter monetary policy weakened underlying economic fundamentals further, and investors responded with more selling of currencies. The debt crisis demonstrated that governments can decide on their own and at any time to deviate from the fiscal compact—the rules that form the linkage between national policies and keep the system together. For example, on several occasions the Irish government threatened to have bondholders of Irish bank debt face a reduction in their principal, called a *haircut*, in exchange for less strict conditions on the bailout package they received from the European Union (EU). The Finnish government demanded collateral from the Greek government on the bailout loans the Finnish government guaranteed. This collateral was embedded somewhere deep in the legal language of the bailout agreement with Greece but was not regarded as a necessity. In response, Austria, the Netherlands, Slovenia, and Slovakia demanded the same. As discussed in Chapter 2, Greek Prime Minister Papandreou called for a public referendum when Greece was forced by EU partners and the International Monetary Fund (IMF) to implement more fiscal austerity measures to get back on track in order to receive its next bailout payment (*tranche*). The fact that Papandreou called for a referendum without consultation shows that a country can abandon the rules and agreements via a referendum.

Similarly, during the ERM crisis, Denmark called for a referendum to ratify the Maastricht Treaty, which it subsequently rejected. This led to a domino effect in currency markets then, just as it led to a domino effect of selling across bond markets in Europe during the debt crisis based on Papandreou's stunt. The Papandreou situation also led to a standoff, whereas German Prime Minister Merkel and French Prime Minister Sarkozy demanded from Greece that the referendum ballot would include a vote to stay in the EU or not. That is, the Greek public would vote yes or no on adopting additional austerity measures contingent on staying in the EU. This is what is called a *classic game of chicken*. In such a game, there is situation where two parties each want to maximize their goal, but only one can win. As one party maintains its stance, eventually the other party "blinks" and "chickens out." Games of chicken are often played between policy makers, specifically between monetary and fiscal policy makers because at times they have opposing objectives, such as lower unemployment versus higher inflation.

Games of Chicken

There are vast political differences between countries that reflect a lack of leadership direction and decision making. The ERM crisis was colored by a huge division among EU officials on generalized currency realignment. There were games of chicken between the Bundesbank, which refused to cut interest rates, and other central banks, which were forced to tighten monetary policy. As speculative attacks on currencies intensified, other EU officials from countries such as Italy were open to discuss devaluations. As in a game of chicken where two or three parties have a stand-off until at some point one "blinks" and "chickens out," so it was with the Bundesbank, which eventually "blinked" in 1992, over cut interest rates, and allowed the Italian lira to devalue by 3.5 percent against the deutschmark. In the aftermath, this decision was viewed as poorly executed because political hints of more devaluations led to a self-fulfilling spiral of currency attacks.

The current debt crisis has been equally colored by deep divisions between German and French politicians as well as politicians from other countries. There was a string of emergency EU summits from 2009 onward producing numerous "comprehensive solutions" and bailout rescue packages for Greece, Ireland, and Portugal; flexible credit lines for Italy and Spain; and funds to intervene in bond markets and facilitate bank recapitalization. The sequential flow of events became cacophonous in nature when before, during, and after each major summit, European officials would unleash attempts to impress or shock markets with creative alternatives to address the crisis. With the passing of each summit, every proposal was quickly devoured, and markets grew wary of the ability of political leaders to gain control of the situation and market participants and the media became skeptical. From the onset, each EU summit's "big agreement" on measures became self-defeating. And it wasn't just markets' disbelief that EU officials would for once be able for to pull something credible together; the numerous games of chicken also played a central role. The primary game was between the ECB, which insisted on "structural reforms," and the EU, which lacked the political will to create them. This game of chicken also was enshrined into the Lisbon Treaty, which forbids the ECB from financing deficits. Each time market pressure rose, the call on the ECB to provide such financing grew, but the ECB stood pat on government following fiscal discipline. The main legal weaponry the ECB used was Lisbon Treaty Article 123 prohibiting monetary financing of governments.

There also were games of chicken among EU countries. For example, the "Troika" (i.e., EU, ECB, and IMF) pressured Greece to implement fiscal austerity, and Greece, in its turn, delayed such progress close to a crucial bond redemption date when it would run out of money. After numerous negotiations, it always ended up with Greece receiving a tranche from its aid package known as the *transfer payment*. Since the games of chicken involved multiple players, they became increasingly complex, which fits in with the terminology of game theory, such as coordinated parties that cause uncoordinated outcomes. This element is a reflection of the asymmetry within the system.

System Asymmetry

The Transfer Payment was an agreement made by EU partners in 2010 to grant Greece aid and establish the European Financial Stability Fund (EFSF) for future bailouts of other countries. The EFSF is a system of loan guarantees made by participating EMU countries, funded by bond issuance. The bonds are sold to the private sector, and in particular, global central banks from China and Japan represented a significant demand factor because both countries have a stake in the stability of Europe. The EFSF had rules in terms of Troika conditions set on tranche payments, but as the Greek example demonstrates, there was leeway toward fiscal slippage to avoid a disorderly default situation. However, the EFSF merely presented a linkage of national policies under one greater good of Europe, as established in Maastricht, now known as the Lisbon Treaty. The linkage of policies was an agreement but never a central, full-fledged pact that would present a one-size-fits-all governance structure. Instead, the linkage was not seen as full but rather as incomplete. Since the treaty did not represent a fiscal union but rather an incomplete one, the EMU could be called an *incomplete transfer union*. In this union, it was once more two countries that set the rules and conditions for the others, namely, Germany and France, who would have a German-Franco summit before each EU summit so as to agree in principle on newly proposed crisis measures. Like the ERM system, where the German Bundesbank set monetary policy for other central banks, the EFSF system experienced the same $n - 1$ asymmetry. The $n - 1$ means one degrees of freedom that forces others to cooperate and adjust. The asymmetry is reflected in the ECB key capital ratios, the percentage of capital or guarantee contribution of each country to the EFSF. Figure 7.1 shows the percentages of ERM system currencies in the EMU versus the contributions of each country in the EFSF (as well as its successor, the European Stability Mechanism [ESM]). As the figure shows, Germany's share is disproportionate to those of other countries. In part, this is so because of each country's gross domestic product (GDP) and population weight. Because Germany has the largest economy, as well as the largest GDP in per-capita terms, it is Germany that takes the lion's share in the ECB, the euro, the EFSF and ESM, and even before the EMU, the European Currency Unit (ECU). Just how asymmetric the distribution between countries is, the percentages in Figure 7.1 are based on the premise that the imbalances (fiscal and trade) will be limited in a common-currency area. In reality, this is not the case, and so, by having a few countries (e.g., Germany, France, Benelux, Austria, and Finland) controlling all resources to offset imbalances has given fuel to political and economic asymmetry. These countries also have limited resources to fight contagion and frequently display an unwillingness to deploy those resources in full.

	ECU	ECB	EFSF	ESM
Germany	32.70%	18.80%	27.10%	27.10%
France	20.80%	14.20%	20.30%	20.30%
Italy	7.20%	12.50%	17.80%	17.80%
Spain	4.20%	8.30%	11.90%	11.90%
Netherlands	9.50%	3.90%	5.70%	5.70%
Belgium	7.80%	2.50%	3.50%	3.50%
Ireland	1.10%	1.10%	0%	0%
Greece	0.80%	1.90%	0%	0%
Portugal	0.80%	1.75%	0%	0%
Austria	0.00%	1.90%	2.80%	2.80%
Finland	0.00%	1.25%	1.80%	1.80%
Luxembourgh	0.30%	0.20%	0.25%	0.25%

Figure 7.1   Asymmetry compared. Paid-in capital percentage per country. Percentages are based on GDP and population weights.

The Presence of Limited Resources

Another comparison angle with the ERM crisis is the unwillingness of countries to commit unlimited resources to fully stem the contagion. The political measures focused on intervention mechanisms. The EFSF is an example as well of a permanent rescue mechanism, the European Stability Mechanism (ESM). During the summer and fall of 2011, several initiatives were taken to build a firewall to stop contagion.

At the EU summit in July 2011, the political leaders agreed to a plan to deal with the crisis. The following excerpt is taken from the July 21, 2011, EU statement:

a. Finance recapitalization of financial institutions through loans to governments including in non-programme countries
b. Intervene in the secondary markets on the basis of an ECB analysis recognizing the existence of exceptional financial market circumstances and risks to financial stability and on the basis of a decision by mutual agreement of the EFSF/ESM Member States to avoid contagion

This statement speaks to building a firewall to stop the contagion. In fact, the firewall had limits because it presented a debt for a debt solution under point (a) and conditionality to freely intervene under point (b). Thus these measures were further enhanced at the EU summit in October 2011 with the following, again an excerpt taken directly from the October 26, 2011, EU statement:

a. Significant optimization of the resources of the EFSF, without extending the guarantees underpinning the facility. The options agreed will allow the EFSF resources to be leveraged. The leverage effect of both options will vary, depending on their specific features and market conditions, but could be up to 4 or 5, which is expected to yield around 1 trillion euro.

b. Comprehensive set of measures to raise confidence in the banking sector by (i) facilitating access to term-funding through a
coordinated approach at the EU level and (ii) the increase in
the capital position of banks to 9 percent of Core Tier 1 by the
end of June 2012. National supervisors must ensure that banks'
recapitalization plans do not lead to excess deleveraging.

Markets like a trillion-dollar headline, but the leveraged version
of the EFSF had no such impact. The reasons were that the leverage
applied was met with skepticism from investors, who questioned its
effectiveness. The idea was that leverage would be applied through
a first-loss principle of 20 percent on each newly issued government
bond by any of the EMU member states. This meant that an insurance certificate was attached to each bond. Other approaches included
leverage through one or more co-investment funds that would attract
external private capital and a tranching method that would allow for
losses to be shared among the different stakeholders. This was seen as
a collateralized debt obligation (CDO) version of the EFSF. As the
U.S. subprime lending crisis had demonstrated, the complexity of a
CDO was ill-understood. A CDO based on an underlying sovereign
portfolio was seen as even more complex. In fact, the use of such a
fund to purchase government bonds backed by an underlying reference
portfolio consisting of government bonds that was compounded in size
to stem contagion made investors wary. Moreover, since the statement
made no reference to a further extension of guarantees underpinning
the EFSF, this meant that the risk of the leverage was going to be carried mostly by private investors.

However, what caused a liquidation of government bonds that
became self-reinforcing was the demand by the European Banking
Association (EBA) and the EU that core tier 1 banks had to increase
their capital position to 9 percent by the end of June 2012. Government
bonds were once viewed as capital buffers because they were weighted

as 0 percent risk by the Bank of International Settlements (BIS). The sovereign crisis created a stigma for banks to hold vast numbers of government bonds. The banks became preemptive and cautious and started a liquidation cycle of assets to achieve adequate capital levels well ahead of the June 2012 deadline. This was part of the reason why certain banks experienced a kind of "institutional bank run" as the markets quickly figured out which institutions were forced to deleverage toxic assets.

Other preventive measures included the European Stability Mechanism (ESM), which was brought into effect in July 2012 to run parallel with the EFSF for one year; the lowering of interest charged on loans from the EFSF to 3.5 percent; and a bilateral loan to the IMF funded by the European national central banks. In addition, these measures were seen as liquidity solutions, functioning as temporary bridges. During 2011, via numerous summits, fiscal governance was strengthened through a so-called six pack (Six Legislative Proposals to Enforce Stability and Growth Pact) that later was endorsed as a "fiscal compact" to enshrine budget rules into national legislation and a Euro "Plus" Pact to enhance the competitiveness of various countries. Moreover, after many deliberations and rejections by Germany, the EU Commission also proposed the concept of "Stability Bonds" as a first step toward common bond issuance. These were long-run measures that, although constructive in nature, took time to come to fruition.

Despite all these measures, the Euro-zone debt crisis intensified throughout 2011. The reason was that all the measures were complex and difficult to understand; all were tied to strict conditions by three parties, namely the EU, IMF, and ECB; all had embedded subordinate characteristics; and most important, all suffered from limited resources.

The EFSF and ESM were special-purpose vehicle structures with differences in legal voting structure; thus the EFSF had unanimity, the ESM had majority voting. Both structures were seen as having insufficient capacity to truly stem contagion. For one thing, the EFSF had to issue debt in order to raise funds for the loans it would grant to program countries and for the potential interventions it would pursue in sovereign primary and secondary markets. The EFSF AAA rating hinged strongly on France's AAA rating, which after review by the rating agencies was downgraded to AA+, as was the EFSF rating. Without an AAA rating on EFSF bonds, the demand from global central banks began to wane, which added vulnerability. Since EFSF leverage was not achieved via a wholesale funding line to the ECB, but rather through complex features such as the first-loss and tranche method, the private sector had little interest in investing, thus limiting the scope of the fund's firepower.

The ESM was a paid-in, callable capital structure. Although the initial, upfront capital was relatively small (80 billion euros), each country contributed over a period of three to five years, and thus capital payments could go as high as 25 billion euros for countries such as Germany by the time the ESM was fully capitalized. These contributions, as well as the guarantees given on EFSF loans, were contingent government liabilities, and thus Eurostat (the European central statistics bureau) would count those contributions as part of each participating country's national debt. The ESM callable structure also brought about a pyramid-like reconfiguration such that if a country such as Italy were to lose access to markets for government funding and needed to tap the ESM for funds, the other contributing countries would have to contribute incrementally more capital to maintain the ESM's overall lending capacity. Thus there was a government bond supply contamination effect built into the ESM callable capital structure. When the ESM was activated, it meant that Germany, France, and the Netherlands, as well as Spain and Italy, would have to issue more government bonds to back bailout funds the ESM had provided to Greece, Ireland, and Portugal. If for some reason Spain were to access the ESM because of market access loss, then all the other member countries would have to issue more government bonds to back the bailout for Spain. As more capital was needed to back ESM loans, more ESM bonds would have to be issued at the same time that member nations would need to issue more sovereign bonds to pay for the ESM capital. The ESM bonds would have collective action clauses (CACs), but they were junior to ESM loans; that is, the ESM had a greater embedded speculative incentive structure than the EFSF.

Germany, as the largest contributor to the EFSF and ESM, had a built-in political barrier to avoid being on the hook for more capital: It demanded a longer payment time (up to five years) to make its entire capital contribution to the ESM, and its contribution to the EFSF was to be capped as well. Capital contributions to the ESM also had to be ratified by the majority of national parliaments. In the case of Germany, it had to be approved by the Constitutional Court, and thus its full capitalization wasn't achieved from day one. These are some of the reasons why the firepower of the ESM was limited.

The EFSF (and ESM) was an implicit corridor system shaped by a lending rate of 3.5 percent and a borrowing rate of around 2 to 3 percent. The lending rate was agreed on by the EU partners, and thus loans were collateralized by guarantees. The EFSF funding rate, however, was market-based via the issuance of bonds. EFSF bonds were "guaranteed" by being ECB repo-eligible collateral, whereas global central banks from China, Japan, and others pledged support by purchasing up to 40 percent of EFSF issuance, according to the EFSF-published breakdown of participating investors. In order not to have imminent default on existing debt (and EFSF loans), Greek, Portuguese, and Irish banks would take down their government's bill auction or government-guaranteed bonds (Ireland) and repo those to the ECB. All these factors revolved around the fact that the EFSF system was set in place for two purposes: (1) to prevent contagion and (2) to achieve a muddle-through scenario until the end of 2012, when the ESM could initiate an "orderly" restructuring through collective action clauses. The EFSF and ESM borrowing and lending mechanisms were aimed at funding bailouts, bank recapitalizations, and bond market interventions. Nevertheless, the system so far has been seen as limited, as evidenced by the continued widening of European sovereign bond spreads relative to the EFSF lending and borrowing rates. In fact, when measures were put in place to address contagion, even by narrowing the EFSF corridor from 7 percent initially to a 3.5 percent lending rate relative to an approximately average 3 percent borrowing rate, yields on Italian, Spanish, Portuguese, Irish, and Greek bonds kept rising. As crisis after crisis followed, a narrower corridor didn't help, even though it represented financing relief for countries that needed aid. A narrower EFSF corridor also was the result of an exchange—lower financing cost for countries needing bailout funds were predicated on adherence to stricter budget rules and austerity. Analogous to the ERM system, where the width of exchange-rate bands was set to be narrow (±2.25 percent [±6.5 percent for Italy]) with the aim of providing disciplined convergence of budgets, debt, and inflation, the EFSF system, aside from being seen as asymmetrical, also was seen as being too rigid in terms of credible criteria that were in sync with economic reality.

Another limitation of the EFSF system was its funding structure in relation to the ECB. The EFSF did not have a banking license and was not allowed to fund itself through the central bank because that would constitute direct financing of government deficits, which is restricted by the Lisbon Treaty (Article 123). EFSF funding is through the capital markets, but it has an indirect character. When the EFSF provides a loan tranche to Greece, for example, the tranche is funded by EFSF bonds sold on the capital markets, where the main investors are European banks and foreign central banks. On the other hand, the ECB purchases Greek government bonds from European banks and provides liquidity to banks with its long-term refinancing operations (LTROs). The ECB so far has been able to redeem its 2010, 2011, and 2012 maturity Greek bond holdings at par because those bonds were funded by EFSF loan tranches as part of the EU and IMF programs.

The ECB provided an additional incentive through its three-year LTRO funding that banks used in part to buy EFSF bonds as collateral. Thus, indirectly, the ECB bond purchases get redeemed by EFSF loans that, in turn, are funded by EFSF bonds purchased by banks that use ECB LTRO funding. Figure 7.2 attempts to describe this funding channel. As the arrows back and forth between the ECB, EFSF, and banks show, at face value it may look like a self-financing system. However, it has ringtones of what can cause domino-style effects. The vulnerability lies in the fact that the EFSF can lose market access when sponsorship by global central banks and European commercial banks is insufficient to cover the increasing EFSF issuance needed to fund more bailout loans. Another weakness is that the ECB has to carry more credit risk on its balance sheet via repo agreements as well as bond purchases. Although that risk is shared by all national central banks against their capital and reserve funds, the collateral backing the repo agreement can be made up of near-default-trading government bonds or EFSF bonds that back EFSF loans that carry the risk of a country on the brink of bankruptcy. The EFSF and ESM are capitalized by non-EU and IMF bailout countries that face increasing funding needs as the twin deficits worsen. The diagram in Figure 7.2 looks to be Ponzi-like, but a better analogy is a "snowball effect," where the worsening of deficits triggers a need for more EFSF loans funded by more EFSF bonds that are financed by more ECB LTROs. The credit risk circles round and round until, at a certain point, the circle breaks.

Thus the markets saw the EFSF/ESM corridor with its EU/IMF/ ECB conditions as too rigid, and this explains why fiscal austerity had little credibility—the conditions and criteria were not aligned with the underlying economies. Despite efforts to adjust this alignment with structural reforms, such reforms take considerable time to implement and bear fruit. The more tightening there was of fiscal measures, the more the EFSF system came under strain. This strain was exacerbated by the view of EU officials that the private sector somehow had to

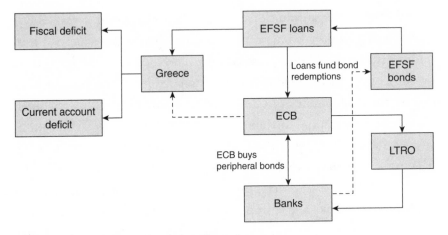

Figure 7.2   Indirect twin-deficit financing.

share the burden of losses in the future and their official creation of specific and unique cases. By pursuing such a road, the aim to separate countries to make them distinct from one another becomes counterintuitive because markets by their nature will price-in a more permanent risk premium that becomes almost impossible to reverse. This is an example of a structural domino effect.

Separation

Restructuring-type measures were aimed at setting a firewall between Greece versus Ireland and Portugal and then another between Portugal and Ireland versus Italy and Spain. Italy and Spain were viewed as systemic to the Euro-zone economy and the broader banking system. A loss of market access by either country not only would deplete the resources that the EU had left in the EFSF and ESM, but it also would mean a severe financial crisis across Europe owing to the large and widespread Italian and Spanish debt holdings in European banks. The systemic nature of the crisis also was expressed by European Union President Herman van Rompuy, who said openly in July 2011 that it was ridiculous to compare Italy and Spain with Greece. The EU summit of July 21, 2011, stated the separation explicitly: "As far as our general approach to private-sector involvement in the euro area is concerned, we would like to make it clear that Greece requires an exceptional and unique solution." This was further solidified in a December 9, 2011, statement: "We clearly reaffirm that the decisions taken on 21 July and 26 and 27 October concerning Greek debt are unique and exceptional."

By formally making Greece a unique and separate case from others, EU officials hoped that the extraordinary measures they had to take to keep Greece from bankruptcy would not have to be repeated for other countries. The stated objective was to draw a line between countries so that financial markets would treat them as individual cases and treat contagion within the means available. *The Economist* in July 2011 termed this "fire fighting"—a localized way to treat contagion. This implied that the lines drawn were rather slim and backed by balance sheets from the EFSF, ESM, IMF, and ECB that were accessible only with significant conditionality, by definition, a constraint. Investors around the world saw this as a limitation in firepower to stem the crisis effectively. Thus bonds from Italy and Spain, as well as France, Austria, and other countries, saw liquidations by, for example, Asian investors, who had made a "permanent" decision to reduce their exposure. Figure 7.3 shows when these investors started changing their minds, which was around the big summit in July 2011. Since much of the European government debt was held in passive index funds and trust funds across Asia as well as Europe, the debt holders represented investors who were normally there for the long haul, often called *strong hands*. Because these investors lacked the conviction that a comprehensive solution could be reached, a sudden demand shift occurred in which they embarked on a mechanical sell program to liquidate European government bonds from their long-term portfolios. This sale program intensified

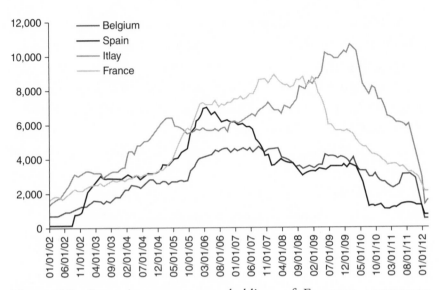

Figure 7.3   Japan investment trust holdings of European government bonds.

(*Source:* The Investment Trust Association of Japan.)

at the same time that Italy faced a political crisis involving Berlusconi and his finance minister, Tremonti, who was seen as a key person to carry out the necessary reforms. As Figure 7.3 shows, the holdings of Italian bonds by Japanese trust funds collapsed, and the demand for the European government bonds shifted permanently. The result was that other investors reacted to this selling by also liquidating their holdings through removal of European countries from their benchmarks and investment guidelines. The demand destruction that took place meant that a generation of future investors would have to be convinced to change their perceptions about the safety of European government bonds, and that would, by necessity, require a massive intervention by European officials. As this analysis shows, the limitations of the EFSF and ESM structures, as well as the unwillingness of the ECB to remove risk from the market in a meaningful way, left the door open for contagion to repeat itself. And that was what occurred during the fall of 2011, when, combined with banks deleveraging out of government bonds in response to the 2012 deadline for capital requirements, there was a significant widening of all sovereign bond spreads, and even countries such as the Netherlands saw rising yields. The liquidity problem had become a broad solvency issue.

The domino effect that unfolded was a flight to quality into German bunds, U.K. gilts, and U.S. Treasuries, as well as Australian government bonds. Their yields fell sharply, whereas those of Spain and Italy rose sharply. Multiple equilibria became visible as the self-fulfilling element of mechanical sales programs led to further selling and liquidations. A classic "run on the bank" now happened to European governments, where investors no longer believed that they could be solvent and so demanded higher rates, which in the case of Greece, Ireland, and Portugal led to a market-driven default. Germany, the United States, and the United Kingdom, despite their debt levels, were seen as solvent, and the markets rewarded those countries with the ability to borrow at a low, riskless rate. The distinction element shows up as well, because countries with higher debt levels travel a smaller distance between solvency and default which in the process narrows the distance between the interest rate associated with solvency and the interest rate associated with default. The demand collapse caused a sharp reversal in the euro–Japanese yen exchange rate as the yen carry trade by borrowing yen and reinvesting in European government bonds unwound.

A Unique Case: Greece

European and Greek officials have been entangled in a series of negotiation twists over further spending cuts to achieve debt sustainability over the course of the debt crisis. Since July 2011, through several tense moments of near-crucial Greek bond redemption dates, the final stages were set for the Greek economy by early 2012. On the one hand, by delivering on spending cut promises and committing to them in writing with its EU partners, the Greek economy actually experienced some stabilization in terms of reaching a primary surplus. From a deficit in 2009 of 10.4 percent of GDP, the primary surplus could reach +0.2 percent of GDP in 2012 and 2013, owing to value-added tax hikes and wage cuts. Despite all the negative news on Greece, it is worth noting that not many countries so far have been able to reach a primary surplus.

At the same time, because the cuts were so draconic, the impact on Greek society will be significant, especially since more than half the working population is employed in the public sector. According to the Greek Statistical Authority, Greek output fell more sharply (–7 percent) on the year in the fourth quarter of 2011, a stark reminder that the Greek GDP has been contracting since the middle of 2008 and has reached 16 percent below its precrisis peak. With more austerity demands layered on top of the economy, the situation in Greece often has been compared with that of Argentina and Latvia. In both cases, the economies from peak to trough experienced an output collapse of between 20 and 25 percent before staging a recovery.

Since the Greek economic sentiment is deteriorating quickly, the challenge remained to execute and implement austerity measures against a backdrop of growing resistance by the Greek people. There was the risk that the agreed-on fiscal targets will become little more than "paper targets" as the economy declines too quickly, making it impossible for Greece to keep up with those targets. The situation was exacerbated by political backtracking on the implementation of reforms, including cutting back on pensions and defense spending. Greece could not count on swift privatization of public-sector assets either. With the Greek downturn lasting twice as long as the average crisis, the interest burden of public debt is expected to rise to 6.3 percent of GDP by 2013, whereas unemployment is forecasted to soar to 20 percent. According to World Bank estimates, Greek GDP could decline as much as 25 to 30 percent by 2013.

Thus the so-called fiscal devaluation that Greece has to cope with in the absence of independent monetary policy and domestic currency depreciation leaves two options to muster economic growth: wage deflation and debt restructuring. Neither is a choice that represents a stable outcome, but either has become a must for Greece. Internal devaluation is possible when one looks at Ireland and Latvia, but in the case of Greece, the political and social aspects have a different dynamic. Greece exiting the currency union doesn't bode well because it will likely force the country's economy into chaos given that its large euro-denominated liabilities (close to 350 billion euros) will have to be redenominated into drachmas.

The rejection by EU partners of a Greek exit from the EMU or a sudden, "hard" default on Greek debt makes the muddle-through scenario most plausible. This is a scenario based on forced economic and social adjustment that will go on for years until all Greek debt is restructured and competitiveness has returned. The Greek economy has reached the final stage, entrenching the reality of a long era of painful economic conditions. The risks remained high, especially when the general elections resulted in further fragmentation of the Greek parliament, which affected elections in June 2012, when a new political movement rejected outright the austerity demanded by the EU, even though it has been signed and committed. Greece therefore remained a catalyst for continuation of the crisis, a repetition of the wakeup call that investors in government bonds can change their perceptions and loyalties.

Embedded Subordination

As the Euro-zone debt crisis engulfed more member states, the notion on the part of Germany and France grew that complex measures to address the crisis entailed in some measure a method to achieve an orderly form of debt restructuring. On insistence by Germany and France during the Pact of Deauville in October 2010, when the

foundations of a permanent rescue mechanism were built, the condition was set that sovereign bondholders would share in future bailouts.
This became known as the *bail-in clause*. A distinction was made
between existing debt and new debt, explicitly worded in the EU statement of November 28, 2010: "In all cases, in order to protect taxpayers' money, and to send a clear signal to private creditors that their
claims are subordinated to those of the official sector, an ESM loan will
enjoy preferred creditor status, junior only to the IMF loan."

An additional feature in this statement was a debt sustainability
test conducted by the European Commission and the IMF in liaison
with the ECB. If the test determined that a country was at risk of
insolvency, the EMU member state had to negotiate a comprehensive
restructuring plan with its private-sector creditors. This plan had to be
in line with IMF practices, with a view toward restoring debt sustainability. In order to facilitate an orderly restructuring process, standard-
ized and identical collective action clauses (CACs) were included on
all newly issued government bonds as of the start of 2013. The CACs
would enable creditors to pass a qualified majority decision to agree to
a legally binding change in the terms of payment of the bond contract.
Such a change could be achieved by maturity extension, a cut in the
coupon interest, or a haircut in the notional value of the bond. The EU
encouraged EMU member states to strive to lengthen the maturities of
their future debt term structure to avoid refinancing peaks and large
bond redemption humps.

Along the same line, the European Commission released a consultation paper in early January 2011 that discussed the degree senior
and subordinated bank debt holders could share in future bailouts of
financial institutions by 2013 to save taxpayers from burden sharing
and to avoid moral hazard. The EU commission stated this as follows:

> Fair burden sharing by means of financing mechanisms which avoid
> use of taxpayer funds. This might include possible mechanisms to write
> down appropriate classes of the debt of a failing bank to ensure that its

creditors bear losses. Any such proposals would not apply to existing bank debt currently in issue. It also includes setting up resolution funds financed by bank contributions. In particular, the Consultation seeks views on how a mechanism for debt write down (or "bail-in") might be best achieved, and on the feasibility of merging deposit guarantee funds with resolution funds.

The financial markets took these future haircuts and subordination to be extremely negative. The fact that existing debt holders were going to be subjected to different debt-restructuring rules from future debt holders whereas future bond holders would be subjected to sharing in losses ignited a domino-style selloff across European government bond markets. On top of this came the European Commission's consultation paper on senior bank debt haircuts that strengthened the speculative incentive for existing senior and subbank debt holders to liquidate their holdings well ahead of when such requirements were to come into effect. This became a catch-up effect in sovereign spreads. After the first Greek crisis of May 2010, the Ireland spread to Greece narrowed until the Irish crisis unfolded. Subsequently, the Portugal spread to Ireland started to narrow until Portugal reached a crisis point, and from then on, slowly but surely, Italy caught up with Portugal by reaching a crisis in July–August 2011. As the catch-up effect continued, like a chain reaction, more structural debt holders exited on the premise of being faced with downgrades and subordination versus future debt based on the bail-in rules.

A Two-Tiered Market

Another implication of embedded subordination is that the CACs, the preferred credit status (albeit watered down for Greece, Ireland, and Portugal in June 2011), the private-sector involvement, and the first-loss insurance of 20 percent on new issuance are all measures that would make the European government bond market a two-tiered market. One the one hand, existing debt is subjected to a different set of rules and will trade at a risk premium to newly issued bonds. The new bonds have more protection from first-loss insurance but also are subjected to restructuring risk by the EU, which will use the CACs as a means to force a bail-in by the private sector. Existing bonds issued under local law with no CACs will be subjected to greater domestic political risk. In such a case, a government has the flexibility to restructure its debt in the manner its wants and when it wants.

The combination of bank debt burden-sharing proposed by the European Commission and the ESM on sovereign debt agreed to in early 2011 set the stage for a repeat of the ERM crisis in the months that followed, leading to a mini bank crisis during the summer into fall of 2011. This was the result of a double layer because the banks that issued senior debt also held significant amounts of government debt. Coupled with accelerated downgrades on both bank and sovereign debt, banks became preemptive and started to liquidate their sovereign bond holdings in a further deteriorating, illiquid market. This illiquidity effect was exacerbated by the same banks that scaled back market-making risk in government bonds. With an additional incentive to withdraw wholesale funding to other banks, the ECB had to intervene by buying not just more sovereign bonds from Italy and Spain but also by extending the maturity of its LTROs into 2014. The asymmetry of the system grew, and the $n - 1$ problem became an $n - 1$ problem squared. It was the catch-up game of speculative incentives between both private- and public-sector debt.

There was another dimension as to why policy resolutions such as the ESM and EFSF made the crisis self-validating. This was that the ESM created a restructuring rank order. This occurred because its structure of callable capital commitment has the potential of incrementally increasing a country's stock of debt each time the country has to access the ESM. This enticed speculation on haircuts of existing debt. Such speculation in November 2010 when Ireland was bailed out resulted in risk premiums on Spanish debt initially lagging but then catching up with Ireland as senior debt holder haircut rumors intensified. When the Portugal bailout came to the fore, it was surrounded by Greek restructuring commentary. Such commentary became a major influence in 2011 that led to an ongoing negotiation of how to "soft restructure" Greece's large government debt.

Soft Restructuring

The subordinated feature that allows a form of restructuring was addressed in 2011 by voluntary rollover and reprofiling terminology that entered the media and economists' debate when it became clear that Greece was well behind in implementing reforms and meeting EU and IMF fiscal targets. It was first ex-ECB board member Bini Smaghi who hinted in a May 2011 interview with the *Financial Times* at such voluntary rollover as part of a new aid package for Greece: "A 50-50 distribution between official and private contributions, with the official part being one-third IMF and two-thirds Euro area countries. For the private component, it would entail partly of privatizations and securitizations, some roll-over of positions in particular by Greek banks and some short-term issuance."

Soon EU officials openly encouraged governments and banks to engage in a "Vienna-style Initiative" to roll Greek bonds with supposed backing of the ECB. The Vienna Initiative was enacted in 2009 in Eastern Europe to prevent a large-scale and uncoordinated withdrawal of cross-border bank groups from a region, which could trigger systemic bank crises by ensuring that parent bank groups publicly committed to maintain their exposures and recapitalize their subsidiaries as part of the overall balance-of-payments support to countries by the IMF and EU.

Because a similar type of Vienna Initiative in the Euro zone came into doubt, another acronym became part of discussions at EU summits and in EU statements—private-sector involvement (PSI). At first, this was put forward by the International Institute of Finance, which stated on July 1, 2011:

> The private financial community is ready to engage in a voluntary, cooperative, transparent and broad-based effort to support Greece given its unique and exceptional circumstances. The involvement of private investors will complement parallel official financing and liquidity support and will be based on a small number of options. These options include a roll-over or extension of maturities and reinvestment of creditor claims into long-dated instruments with principal collateralization. In addition, it would be important to consider possible debt buyback proposals.

Many proposals started to address how to roll over Greek bonds. One proposal by French banks "agreed to roll [over] Greek sovereign debt maturing from mid-2011 to mid-2014 around 70 cents on the dollar, whereby half of the amount was to be into new 30-year Greek securities, and the remaining 20 percent invested in a fund made of very high quality securities backing the new 30-year Greek bonds." The new 30-year Greek debt would carry an interest rate of 5.5 percent with a bonus element linked to Greek growth of up to an additional 2.5 percent per annum, making the maximum interest rate 8 percent on Greek debt. This proposal would imply a soft haircut of 21 percent from par on Greek bonds. After much tossing and turning, the initial voluntary haircut set on Greek debt was 21 cents at the July 21, 2011, EU summit. The PSI for Greece was officially announced at that summit: "The financial sector has indicated its willingness to support Greece on a voluntary basis through a menu of options further strengthening overall sustainability."

The Institute for International Finance addendum was attached to the EU statement that explained the menu of options in more detail: (1) A par bond exchange into a 30-year instrument, (2) a par bond offer involving rolling over maturing Greek government bonds into 30-year instruments, (3) a discount bond exchange into a 30-year instrument, and (4) a discount bond exchange into a 15-year instrument. In each case, it was assumed that "investors would select among the four instruments in equal proportions of 25 percent of total participation," and all the "instruments will be priced to produce a 21 percent net present value (NPV) loss based on an assumed discount rate of 9 percent."

At first, this finance offer to Greece looked to be promising, but soon it turned out not to be sufficient because the total new package for Greece at an additional 130 billion euros financed by the EU and the IMF (66–33 percent split) couldn't be fully financed with a combination of privatization proceeds and a PSI agreement. Mainly because the PSI required a high participation rate of close to 90 percent, the offer wasn't entirely achievable unless the ECB would participate with its Greek holdings (estimated at 45 billion euros) as well. Former ECB President Trichet vehemently resisted the notion because if the ECB were to participate in the rollover, it would lose its independence. The opinion of the rating agencies was that the high participation rate needed would no longer make the PSI voluntary but rather coercive, which would place Greece ratings at selective or restrictive default.

The EU negotiated a collateral guarantee with the ECB so that the central bank could continue to accept Greek bonds once they would fall into selective default. When the Greek economy continued to deteriorate in 2011 and Greece kept falling behind on its fiscal targets, the notion among EU officials grew that the PSI haircut had to go beyond 21 percent. Greek bond prices started to fall, and this spilled over to other markets, such as Italy. This is a combination of self-fulfilling ideas: Confidence in bond markets was sapped and liquidity conditions deteriorated while officials called for further deep haircuts on the part of bondholders and fiscal targets appeared not to be credible along with political wrangling.

These factors set European banks in motion in that they saw basically that the writing was on the wall. Having large exposures to Italian and Spanish government debt, funding pressures started to further creep into the European banking system. As the EBA stress tests of June 2011 revealed, European banks started to liquidate their Italian and Spanish government bond holdings on a grand scale. Taking from the 2011 EBA stress test, Figure 7.4 shows how much that entailed per major bank. One of the main reasons for this was that banks holding sovereign bonds that were viewed as toxic saw their share prices decline, which, in turn, forced those banks to sell more sovereign holdings. During the summer and fall of 2011, this created an asset liquidation spiral akin to Irving Fisher's deleveraging cycle.

The complexity of the PSI negotiations grew as it was revealed that the Greek government debt spread among foreign investors involved in a wide variety of interests and stakes in the process. According to Bloomberg data, Greek government debt had an average maturity of seven years, and despite the fact that its average coupon interest was 4.8 percent, the yields on current Greek bonds ranged from 25 percent

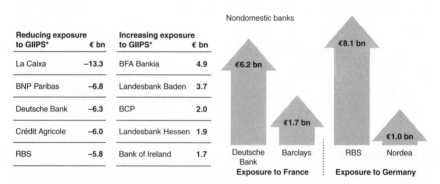

Figure 7.4   Bank deleveraging set in motion during the second and third quarters of 2011. European banks sovereign exposure. Change in sovereign holding (Q4 2010–Q3 2011)
* Greece, Ireland, Italy, Portugal, and Spain.
(*Source: Financial Times,* using data from EBA.)

for 30-years bonds to astronomically high levels of 55 to 75 percent on short-term bonds. Some of these bonds, having just a few months left before they matured, appeared to be held by a wide variety of private parties as well as the ECB. As the PSI discussions continued, it became clear that some of the private-sector investors were not that convinced of the need to roll over their short-dated bonds because they expected to receive par back. This was based on the idea that Germany and other countries would continue to make tranche payments to Greece. These tranche payments in a sense allowed for smooth redemptions of Greek debt. The investors who held short-term Greek bonds were called *holdouts*. There also were *free riders*, parties who bought short-term Greek bonds at a low discount. They also had a similar objective as the holdouts—to benefit from the EU aversion to a disorderly default in Greece.

The holdouts and free riders added further complexity. There was the ECB, which held approximately 45 to 50 billion euros notional of Greek bonds (according to estimates by several primary dealer firms). The ECB was seen a "special" creditor because its bond holdings, purchased under its Securities Market Program (SMP), received preference over those of other bondholders. The reason was that the ECB did not want to participate in the PSI because it did not want to be involved as a public entity in private-sector negotiations. Another backdrop is that the ECB did want to give an incentive to other governments to follow the route of PSI and backtrack on their reforms (if the central bank were to roll over its Greek holdings). The fact is that if the ECB were to do so, it essentially was backing the PSI, something it had opposed early on and warned that it did not present a viable solution to achieve fiscal sustainability. And so the private sector, the ECB, and the rating agencies stood opposed to one another. As some of those private-sector participants either attempted to free ride or held out, Greek officials put forward an incentive by retroactively introducing of CACs on existing Greek bonds. In Greek courts, the clauses can be

introduced fairly easily by a vote in parliament. These clauses, depending on how precisely they are inserted in legal documents, can alter
the terms of existing bonds materially, and the free riders may be faced
with deeper haircuts on their notional bond holdings after all. Such an
introduction of CACs, however, was seen by the rating agencies as a
coercive measure that potentially could lead to a default rating.

The negotiations were colored by a continuous debate about the
appropriate coupon on new bonds that ultimately would determine
the final NPV loss bond holders would take. The PSI as a unique,
technical, and complex solution was meant to be a one-off. In reality, the PSI process since July 2011 slowly converged the bond price
of short-dated Greek bonds toward the price of long-dated Greek
bonds. This illustrates a behavior among various stakeholders that
resembled in a sense cajoling or even arm-twisting on the part of
both the private and the public sectors. There also was the innova-
tion factor—the fact that financial engineering made it possible for
certain bond holders to be uninsured; that is, they sit at the negotiating table but have no real say in the decisions and no stake in the
game. However, their interest was to collect on the credit default swap
(CDS) insurance they bought, and thus a restructuring of Greek debt
would be to their advantage if it was a credit event. A *credit event*
occurs when the specific protection provided by a CDS is triggered.
The ECB's position during the PSI process was notable. The ECB
stood pat on that idea that if the banks were to take an NPV loss of
50 percent or higher, it should be done without the CDS contracts
being triggered by a credit event. One explanation was that banks
had bought sovereign default insurance en masse. A second explanation was that the ECB, intimately familiar with the financial system,
also knew its greatest weakness—a lack of transparency. With this
in mind, the ECB may have known that investors were unable to
gauge the impact of a forced default that could cause a credit market
freeze. On the other hand, the ECB was perhaps also aware of the

few large banks that wrote default insurance contracts and, in case of sudden Greek default, would be deemed systemically important. As it became evident that the ECB Greek bond holdings would be subject to insertion of CACs because they did not participate in the PSI, the ECB and Greece organized a debt swap. This was a technical procedure whereby the original ECB bond holdings were changed for the same bonds with a different registration number (called ISIN), and those securities would not be subjected to CACs.

There were two significant results from ECB's participation in the PSI. The ECB was able to realize profits on its Greek holdings, with the new bonds marked at par versus its current holdings marked at the cost price. The profits were channeled to Euro-zone governments via their respective national central banks in the form of dividend payments. The debt swap created a separate bond class that made the ECB's new holdings senior to existing holdings because they were isolated from the exercise of CACs. Greece was able to call for the CACs on the old bonds, and still their activation did not force any potential loss on the ECB because there would be no aggregation of old bonds and new bonds issued to the ECB. Investors were no longer able to comfort themselves with thinking that the exercise of CACs was unlikely, and that made a voluntary PSI more likely, and the participation rate rose given that there was a credible CAC threat. The Greek government voted the CACs into law and set the threshold for PSI participation lower at 66 percent in order to further incentivize the holdouts to go along with the PSI. A 66 percent threshold is the same threshold for U.K. law bonds issued before 2004, whereas after 2004, U.K. law–issued sovereign bonds usually have a 75 percent threshold. While offering the PSI terms, Greece could have asked those who agreed to participate to sign up for negative consent and use that to call the remaining bonds at much more onerous terms because such "coercion" would have incentivized high participation in the PSI. The PSI terms of ECB also changed in

February 2012, whereas total notional value of bonds exchanged became 53.5 percent (from 50 percent agreed on in October 2011), an average coupon of 3.6 percent for average maturity of 30 years, and the total NPV loss for private investors became 73 to 74 percent, as reflected by the new offer made by the Institute of International Finance. The worse PSI terms and the ECB holdings being senior to existing debt claims because they were not subjected to CACs essentially called into question the effectiveness of the SMP program because the bonds it purchased always could get preferential treatment in a debt-restructuring situation.

The other implication was the co-financing agreement between Greece and the EFSF. The newly created Greek government bonds under the new terms of the PSI agreement would be for a total outstanding amount of around 62 billion euros. This was based on an expected participation rate of 95 percent and a share of 31.5 percent of newly created Greek bonds in the 53.5 percent notional bond exchange. The co-financing arrangement in conjunction with the EFSF was a 30 billion euro loan to Greece that also would fund the PSI cash sweeteners in the form of EFSF notes. The purpose was to align the timing of interest and principal payments between the existing and newly created Greek bonds and to allow for a pro-rata sharing and equal treatment of the newly created Greek bonds with the loan from the EFSF. This complex way of funding meant that whenever there would be a coupon or principal payment on the newly created Greek bonds, a payment also was made to the EFSF loan. An embedded risk was that if Greece were not able to pay its obligations to holders of the newly created Greek bonds, it also would not be able to repay the EFSF loan obligation. The IMF debt sustainability analysis on Greece published in February 2012 said the following about this co-financing agreement: "The PSI deal, in the process of being agreed with creditors, has worsened the outlook for new market access due to the proposed co-financing structure with the EFSF (which essentially implies that any new debt will be junior to all existing debt). It is now uncertain whether market access can be restored in the immediate post-program years." The EFSF loans to fund the PSI cash component became junior to the other EFSF loans that were be provided to Greece for budget and bailout purposes.

Another element of political significance was that once the ECB tipped over to facilitate the PSI, other countries such as Ireland and Portugal took notice. Irish Finance Minister Noonan said, for example, on February 8, 2012: "If the ECB are prepared to make this kind of concession to Greece, it would encourage me to think that they might be ready to make concessions on the promissory note to Ireland. I see it, if it occurs, as a strengthening of our negotiating position." This example was displayed many other times during the crisis. This was a "human" element of a self-centered approach, where one country received an advantage from the EU partners, and others noticed and attempted to get the same through pattern bargaining of dynamic games of chicken. This element of the crisis plays very much into the financial domino theory's cornerstone—inspiring to emulate.

The effect of the lengthy PSI negotiations showed not just convergence between short- and long-dated Greek bond prices, but also bond prices reaching the destination of the outcome of the PSI—a haircut (NPV loss) of 73 to 75 percent from par. There were two domino effects at work. The first was the success of the PSI, setting in motion expectations of replication elsewhere. Although in a different agreement, the PSI success would be viewed as orderly restructuring and therefore a solution for countries to deal with a debt burden. The other effect was the expectation that the PSI would not be successful enough to provide sufficient debt relief, with a potential spillover to other countries that experienced slippage in reaching fiscal targets. Since the PSI was viewed as a unique situation, countries that fell behind because of economic weakness and needed more funding remained subject to a disorderly restructuring process risk. When CACs were introduced on future new government bonds, the existing government debt remained without such clauses. Then, without an effective PSI framework, restructuring risk was a self-fulfilling outcome. Domino effects stemming from these events consisted of further forced liquidations owing to rating downgrades to junk levels and benchmark guideline adjustments. As the crisis entered its third year, that financial domino effect risk remained.

Standard & Poor's (S&P's) head of sovereign ratings John Chambers said the following about Greece on January 24, 2012: "It's not given that Greece default would have a domino effect in the Euro zone." In the context of the complexity of the Greek PSI process, S&P's statement was brought into question. On the one hand, there were the stakeholders who had invested in U.K. law bonds. As mentioned earlier, U.K. law bonds have CACs that require 66 percent (for bonds issued prior to 2004) to 75 percent (for bonds issued after 2004) of bondholders to modify contract terms that would make them binding on others. These bondholders presented a potential blocking vote in the restructuring process. On the other hand, the local law bondholders are at the mercy of the issuer, which could change the terms of the bond contract in local court at any time. Local law bonds require 100 percent of holders to participate to make a change in the bond contract voluntary. Local law bonds can be changed under local jurisdiction which may result in a coercive change of the bond contract otherwise known as "cram-down upon all creditors." Each case presents holdouts, parties who can force the restructuring process one way or the other via block voting. The risks of the restructuring process between local and UK law bond holders had domino effect elements as well. There is a nuisance value that is defined as 33 percent or greater of the vote. Under U.K. law, such a vote can block the entire restructuring, including local law–issued bonds. There is a mopping-up law, where a supermajority can accept a change to bond payment terms that makes it binding for others, specifically the holdouts. Another term is *litigation arbitrage*, where adverse claims can be filed in international litigation, and even central banks could be sued. A side litigation class was called *fraudulent conveyance*, and it implied that a central bank or official entity such as the IMF that provided financing to a sovereign in default had priority debt over other claims. This could further subordinate local and U.K. law existing claims. And last, there was a notion that there could be *sovereign subordination* when a sovereign forced a cram-down on both U.K. and local law bond holders, which might lead to tranching sovereign debt into senior and junior bonds.

There was a certain fear that even when the PSI was completed, the Greek government could pull a stunt and restructure the remaining local law debt the way it saw fit, even though it would risk permanently damaging its reputation as a future issuer. If the Greek government were to have this option, it could set a precedent for every sovereign issuer. If Greece were to get away with this "stunt," it would set in motion a chain reaction of creditors dumping local law bonds for U.K. law bonds, and subordination between U.K. law bonds and domestic law bonds then would become a fact. The legal details, however, of how CACs would be inserted, how the Greek government could impose indentures on U.K. law debt, and how lengthy litigation processes would be remained an uncertainty. However, the more immediate domino effect would have been in Greece's potential collapse of twin-deficit financing. As explained earlier, Greece's rapidly deteriorating twin deficits were funded by EFSF loans. These loans were funded by EFSF bonds bought by banks and global central banks. The banks used the ECB's LTRO funds to purchase the EFSF bonds. The EFSF loans, in turn, helped to redeem Greek government bonds (including ECB holdings) each time EU/IMF made transfer payments to Greece. This "system" of twin-deficit funding will remain intact as long as (1) the EU and the IMF are willing to redeem Greek bonds with tranche payments to avoid disorderly default, (2) the ECB continues term LTROs, and (3) banks and central banks perceive the risk of EFSF bonds to be limited. The PSI having a cash payment (15 percent) potentially in the form of EFSF bonds and ECB accepting them as collateral guarantee if and when participating in the PSI may have altered the risk/reward ratio of EFSF bonds.

The risk perception of EFSF bonds remained crucial to investors. The ECB's Greek bond holdings brought back the transfer-price issue from early 2011. At an average of 85 cents paid for one- to five-year Greek bonds, about 23 billion Euros was held, according primary dealer surveys. At an average market price of about 25 cents, the remaining 60-cent loss had to be absorbed eventually by someone, either the EFSF directly with bond issuance or recapitalizing the ECB or the national central banks (NCBs) with EFSF collateral. The way that Greece's twin deficits are being funded is somewhat similar to that for Portugal and even, to a degree, for Ireland. If the PSI-type route were to be followed in Ireland and Portugal and if the ECB were to go along in the Greek PSI, it also would entail EFSF collateral being an important part of future debt exchanges. The ECB's Portuguese and Irish bond holdings were purchased at high prices compared with their current market values, and the potential loss that may have to be absorbed by the EFSF (and ESM) in the future would be large. The real domino effect lay with the EFSF's ability to continue to fund the deficits of these three countries. In the absence of material growth, this is something that the market has a high incentive to question.

The Role of the Rating Agencies

It is well known that the rating agencies were far behind the curve by the time the U.S. subprime crisis spun out of control, and in fact, they are seen as part of the cause of the financial crisis. The main argument is that the methodology of the rating agencies in analyzing and rating securitizations based on loss-model projections was seen by market participants as severely flawed. In this sense, the rating agencies were retroactive and reactive. This fact may have a played a role in why the rating agencies became proactive during the sovereign debt crisis. Despite the exposed flaw in their methodologies, the decisions to downgrade numerous Euro-zone countries, as well as the United States, continue to have a significant influence. This influence is fourfold:

1. *Political.* Before and just after each EU summit, the rating agencies would put out statements addressing the credibility and long-run viability of announced measures.
2. *Hardwiring.* Ratings are coded into the government bond benchmark universe and into guidelines and investor mandates.
3. *The risk-free rate.* The downgrade of the United States and the pending downgrades of the remaining AAA countries in Europe has shrunk the universe of the risk-free rate (government bonds rated AAA) to just the United Kingdom, Scandinavia, and Australia.
4. *Rating migration.* As a result of the evolution of downgrades of Euro-zone peripherals, several emerging-market countries such as Brazil, Chile, and Mexico saw upgrades.

Figure 7.5 shows that the rating downgrades followed each other in a sequence, one downgrade after the other, as political disagreement caused brinkmanship and economic deterioration made the rating agencies even more preemptive to downgrade sovereign ratings.

The most profound influence rating downgrades had was on the passive index universe. An index fund replicates the movements of an index of a specific market under a set of rules of constant ownership, whatever the market direction or change in market conditions. A *passive* index fund has a predetermined strategy that doesn't entail any active bets or market timing. These index funds have low investing fees and transaction costs because the funds attempt to avoid failing

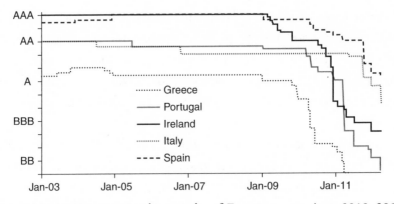

Figure 7.5 Rating agencies downgrades of European sovereigns, 2010–2011.
(*Source:* Bloomberg.)

to correctly anticipate future market changes by instead mimicking the performance of an externally specified index. This index universe is large and estimated by Citigroup to be over $1 trillion. There have been estimates by Citigroup's World Government Bond Index group that at end the end of 2010, the estimated impact of downgrades to junk of Ireland, Portugal, Spain, and Italy on passively managed government bond portfolios would amount to a cumulative total of "forces sales" of $157 billion against Citigroup indices alone. When the forced sales occurred, they would add to the supply on top of the planned issuance. With too much supply in the face of an already scaled back demand by investors, bond prices fall. As they fall and interest rates rise, more investors react.

The Lender of Last Resort

In the spring of 2010, the ECB was looking to start "normalization" of the excess liquidity it had injected into the banking system since 2007. The ECB started a campaign of slowly receding the liquidity by not extending its LTROs with a one-year term and offering more short-term operations with one-week, one-month, or three-month terms. In addition, the ECB reduced the "full allotment" and fixed rate to variable. At the same time, the tensions in the Greek government bond market grew.

Despite repeated calls for the ECB to step into markets and buy government bonds, former ECB President Trichet famously said at the ECB meeting on May 6, 2010, the day before the meltdown in the Greek bond market: "We didn't discuss the matter. I have nothing else to say on that. We call for decisive actions by governments to achieve a lasting and credible consolidation of public finances." Subsequently, on May 10, 2010, the ECB announced a new intervention program, called the Securities Market Program (SMP). This moment became known as a classic U-turn—the fact that a central bank such as the ECB, which is fiercely independent, can adopt measures that to a degree subordinate its independence.

The following excerpts indicate how this program would function: "The Governing Council of the ECB decided on several measures to address the severe tensions in certain market segments which are hampering the monetary policy transmission mechanism and thereby the effective conduct of monetary policy oriented towards price stability in the medium term." The relevance lies in "monetary policy transmission." Whereas the Federal Reserve and the Bank of England quantitative easing (QE) programs were targeted at "portfolio balance," the ECB would conduct this program on the basis that excessive volatility in interest rates would strain the transmission of its policy rate (known as the *refi rate*), particularly on inflationary expectations. As the ECB gradually adjusts its refi rate up or down, it is meant to telegraph monetary policy across the whole of the monetary union, where inflationary expectations are perhaps not fully responded to in a similar, sequential manner. When the Euro-zone debt crisis intensified and interest rates rose abnormally high in Greece, as well as other countries, the effectiveness of policy rate, in the ECB's view, was diminished.

The following section of the May 2010 statement describes the ECB reservation about an "all-in" QE approach to the debt crisis:

In making this decision we have taken note of the statement of the Euro area governments that they "will take all measures needed to meet fiscal targets this year and the years ahead in line with excessive deficit procedures" and of the precise additional commitments taken by some Euro area governments to accelerate fiscal consolidation and ensure the sustainability of their public finances. In order to sterilize the impact of the above interventions, specific operations will be conducted to re-absorb the liquidity injected through the Securities Markets Programme.

Thus this intervention program was not aimed at monetizing government debt to expand the monetary base to alleviate economies from credit contraction by the private sector. The final section explains how interventions would be conducted and its market purpose:

To conduct interventions in the Euro area public and private debt securities markets (the Securities Markets Programme) to ensure depth and liquidity in those market segments which are dysfunctional. The objective of this program is to address the malfunctioning of securities markets and restore an appropriate monetary policy transmission mechanism. The scope of the interventions will be determined by the Governing Council.

The stated objective on monetary transmission also had another method: The intervention had to have a random character to stem sudden volatility in markets. The SMP therefore has been viewed more as a foreign-exchange style of intervention.

The use of elements of surprise, along with the purpose of a foreign-exchange intervention, to stem excessive short-term volatility lead to overshooting of fundamental conditions that might significantly hurt economies. The importance of this comes into play at an intervention level. Another fact is the sterilization of the intervention.

The ECB SMP was ineffective at stemming sovereign debt contagion for the following reasons:

1. *Intervention mechanics.* There was no specific yield or price level the ECB would explicitly target to stem volatility in certain bond markets. The ECB never used aggressive or radical enough tactics, such as a short squeeze, to stop volatility; that is, the ECB bank didn't use its mandate to stand above the law to manipulate markets temporarily. There was only an "anecdotal" yield level at around 6 to 7 percent where the ECB would at times intervene more heavily, but never with unlimited amounts or persistent activity in the market. The SMP interventions therefore also were intramarginal interventions because they specifically targeted "dysfunctional" markets such as that in Greece, where distressed bond prices perhaps breached the lower end of an unknown-to-markets fluctuation margin.

2. *Coordination.* Although coordinated among the Euro-system national central banks, it ended up being the central banks of Germany, France, the Netherlands, Italy, and Spain that carried the burden of the intervention. It was not a globally coordinated intervention with the help of the Federal Reserve, the Bank of Japan, and others, like the Euro exchange-rate intervention in the fall of 2000.

3. *Policy duality.* The instrument of choice (government bonds) had a dual policy objective—fiscal and monetary—that resulted in conflict at times between the ECB and national governments on fiscal governance and structural reform progress.

4. *Governing council division.* The SMP was so controversial that Bundesbank's President Axel Weber and Vice President Jürgen Stark both resigned from the ECB council because they strongly disagreed with the course taken.

These four factors have actually contributed to an extent to failure because the ECB refused to be the lender of last resort. Not only did the ECB frequently used the "Treaty forbids it" argument, but it also was quite explicit in terms of keeping a strict separation between fiscal policy and monetary policy. Figure 7.6 shows the SMP I and SMP II effects, where in both cases basically Greece, Ireland, Portugal, and Italy almost lost market access. What started as a large intervention by the ECB in the first few weeks led to subsequent tapering in purchases even when crucial interest-rate levels of 6 to 7 percent were broken. As a result, during SMP I and SMP II, interest rates kept rising. This was the result of a noncommitment to go all-in, to ensure that sovereign yields were capped below 7 percent, the level where investors made the distinction between interest-rate and credit risk. The bond purchases in the SMP were seen as an insufficient demand backstop that led to the illiquidity of bond markets as market makers scaled back their risk-taking and funding markets for bonds froze. The other cause for failure was that the SMP was not transparent in detail, which left market participants guessing as to how much was purchased, so there was not a true support benchmark measure. As Figure 7.6 once more demonstrates, despite the purchases, the average Greek, Irish, and Portuguese bond yields ended in insolvency territory. In addition, when Italian and Spanish average bond yields went above 7 percent in late 2011, it wasn't the SMP purchases that eventually brought their rates down but rather the LTRO credit easing effect described in Chapter 4.

"Trilemma"

When the ECB began normalizing its monetary policy stance around the middle of 2010, it advocated a "separation policy" between its standard and nonstandard measures. By controlling excess liquidity, the ECB stressed that it could adjust the level of its policy rate while

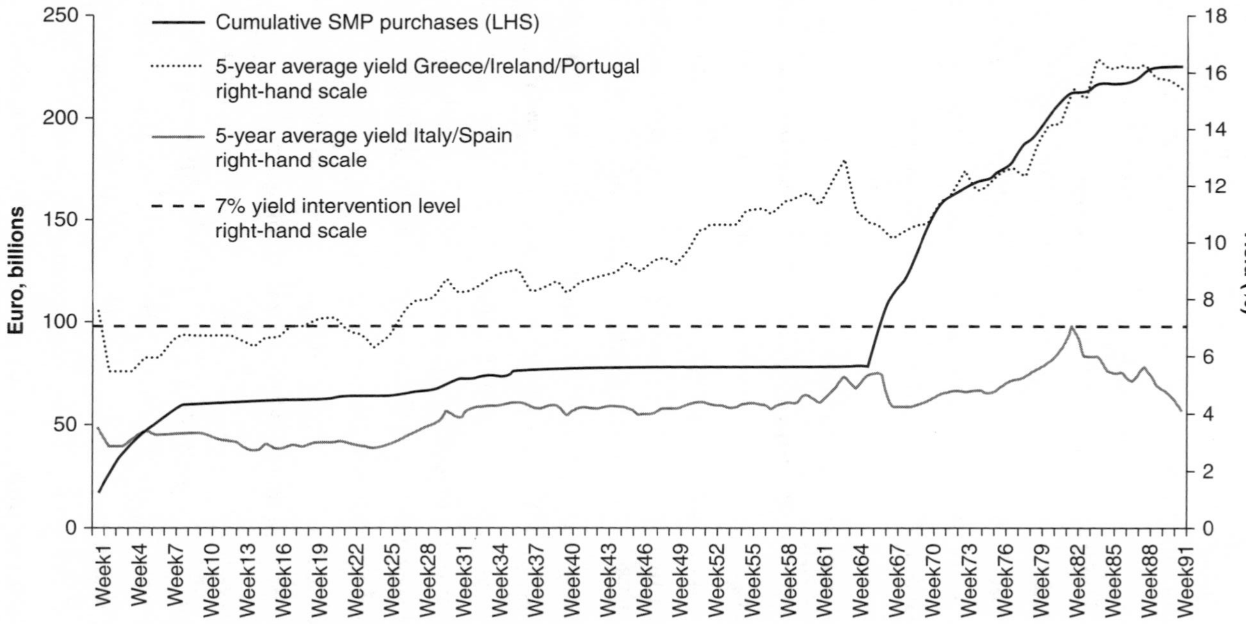
Cumulative SMP purchases (LHS)
5-year average yield Greece/Ireland/Portugal right-hand scale
5-year average yield Italy/Spain right-hand scale
7% yield intervention level right-hand scale
Euro, billions
250
200
150
100
50
0
Yield (%)
18
16
14
12
10
8
6
4
2
0
Week1
Week4
Week7
Week10
Week13
Week16
Week19
Week22
Week25
Week28
Week31
Week34
Week37
Week40
Week43
Week46
Week49
Week52
Week55
Week58
Week61
Week64
Week67
Week70
Week73
Week76
Week79
Week82
Week85
Week88
Week91

Figure 7.6 The SMP effect on sovereign yields.
(*Source:* Bloomberg, ECB.)

easing liquidity conditions simultaneously by lowering its effective policy rate. The difference between standard and nonstandard
policy measures is observed as the "bias" driven by the level of the
effective policy rate, known as the *Euro Over Night Index Average*
(EONIA), a rate that at any time can run at or below the actual
policy rate. The ECB manages the bias within a corridor system
consisting of the policy rate, the lending rate, and the deposit rate.
This is the so-called monetary corridor. The global financial crisis
prevented this by forming a link between the ECB's policy rate and
its nonstandard measures, a link that now has become more deeply
embedded in the construct of the ECB's functioning as a result of
the sovereign debt crisis. This link may have complicated the ECB's
ability to respond preemptively to the acceleration of inflation
because it had to intervene in bond markets to counter speculation over sovereign defaults in peripheral nations. The uncertainties
surrounding Europe's sovereign debt put pressure on the wholesale
funding markets for Europe's banks, which the ECB countered by
providing excess liquidity. The implication, however, was that the
ECB remained confined to its monetary corridor in order to provide sufficient stability to the bond markets. There is an interaction
between the monetary corridor and the EFSF corridor—the *fiscal
corridor*. This corridor, as explained earlier, is the difference between
the EFSF lending rate and borrowing rate.

Each time a crisis occurred, the ECB intervened in the fiscal corridor with bond purchases while maintaining ample liquidity in its
monetary corridor with funding operations. The central bank therefore
had to strike a balance between the two corridors in a way more forced
than was normal. This is essentially a "trilemma" because the ECB had
to stabilize the prices of bonds, consumer goods, and excess liquidity
at the same time. Trying to achieve a balance among all three ultimately can lead to a difficult tradeoff: The ECB must choose whether

to stabilize bond prices by keeping liquidity abundant and perhaps let inflation run above its target rate or otherwise tighten monetary policy significantly to control inflation. Until sovereign default risk was fully stabilized, the ECB had to maneuver delicately between the fiscal and monetary corridors.

The Breakup of the European Monetary Union?

Meeting the convergence criteria demonstrated rigidities in the 1990s, and they became even more challenging in the wake of the 2008 financial crisis. When in May 2010 a financial aid package was formalized for Greece, the EMU convergence criteria became subject to conditions set by the EU and the IMF. It could be argued further that the convergence criteria became applicable to the most fiscally sound countries that not only could meet the criteria in any economic cycle and were committed to do so but also had an economy that could bear tight monetary and fiscal policy. A historical precedent was seen in countries such as Germany, France, Luxembourg, and the Netherlands, which had similar anti-inflation policies, hard currencies, and limited imbalances and were closer to being optimal currency areas prior to EMU. The economies of these countries are open enough to one another to be competitive, and their labor unions have demonstrated a level of flexibility during hard times.

What could happen is a further enhancement of cooperation between their national governments through fiscal governance. This also would mean that the euro as a currency would remain in circulation, and the ECB would determine monetary policy. This also falls within the spirit of the original principles of the Maastricht Treaty that not all countries can join a monetary union. A new core monetary union is likely to be a gradual process but an outcome that the European debt crisis has strengthened. Opting out of the EMU has been debated lately. Multiple scenarios are possible, but each cost/benefit analysis of any country leaving the EMU presents a tradeoff: Bond yields would soar further, currencies would devalue, and payment systems would be severely damaged, offsetting any potential competitive gains to be made. The possibility of forming a new but smaller monetary union has received attention in the media. Specifically, now, bond yields in countries such as Greece, Ireland, and Portugal, as well as Italy, have reached levels where debt can rise exponentially. Without the possibility of an independent lender of last resort printing unlimited currency or successfully implementing labor market reforms to regain competitiveness, restructuring of government debt could become inevitable.

However, there are two "corner solutions" to the European debt crisis:

1. Fiscal union with common bond issuance
2. Debt structuring that includes an exit from the euro

These solutions are mutually exclusive because you can get solution 1 only without solution 2 happening. They are also collectively exhaustive because the crisis has reached a point where (1) fiscal union or (2) restructuring must happen. The condition for either solution 1 or solution 2 to occur is a sequence of events that is mutually inclusive: One event happens only if another event does as well. The probability of a fiscal union or debt restructuring happening therefore is determined by the sum of the probability of mutually inclusive events. So what were these events?

The first event was continuous attempts by politicians to impress the markets. For example, after the alleged "attack" on Italian bonds in July and August of 2011, the Italian lower house of parliament gave final approval to an austerity package that was introduced into the legislature just four days earlier. The second event was that such austerity measures lack credibility in bond markets, so EU officials held emergency summits. Since the summits yielded to more austerity conditions in exchange for loans, this lead to climatic events such as Greek parliamentary votes to approve new austerity measures. Rating agencies repeatedly downgraded each country receiving bailouts, which led to further market pressure, with policy makers trying to impress even further. That is, attempts to impress, emergency summits, austerity votes, and downgrades are all mutually inclusive. This event sequence engulfed Euro-zone countries over the past two years like a brush fire.

Throughout, governments were forced to further link their fiscal policies as directed by two countries, namely, Germany and France. Policy linkage led to the EFSF system, where bailout transfers were funded by ECB repos and global central bank EFSF bond purchases. This is the so-called transfer union, a slow, muddle-through process that may lead to corner solution 1, the fiscal union. The capacity of the EFSF system became politically limited because countries such as Germany and the Netherlands did not want to further increase the size of the fund.

Since the market recognized this capacity constraint early on, confidence in reaching solution 1 changed when contagion spread. To get to a corner solution, another mutually inclusive event had to happen. For corner solutions to be mutually exclusive and collectively exhaustive, the required condition is mutually inclusive events. Former ECB President Trichet said at an ECB July 2011 press conference that engagement in structural reforms hampered by rigidities in EU economies is "the problem of Europe." The events that played throughout the crisis were a reflection of rigidities and hardball politics and could be called "the mutually inclusive problem of Europe."

This problem has reached a stage where markets increasingly discount the possibility of an end game for Europe. If financial markets are right, then as forward looking as they are, they also will discount scenarios showing how the end game could unfold. One widely debated scenario is an exit from the monetary union. The ECB and other academics have published papers on this topic that may offer some insight. A question posed is whether exit from the EMU is mutually agreed on, and thus a new type of ECU (former precursor to the euro) has to be introduced. Barry Eichengreen pointed out several significant costs in an EMU breakup: (1) reversal of the euro payment system, (2) lengthy political debate and passage by national parliaments of treaty changes, and (3) market discounts redenomination of claims in national currencies that causes runs on banks and financial assets. In 2009, the ECB published a study by Phoebus Athanassiou, who argued that a negotiated withdrawal from the EU would be impossible legally, but a unilateral withdrawal would be legally (and politically) controversial. The ECB paper saw an enacted exit clause as not in harmony with the rationale of European unification. Moreover, legally problematic as an exit from the EMU would be, a parallel withdrawal from the EU was viewed as legally impossible by the ECB. The paper concludes, however, that exit from the EMU may not necessarily mean that use of the euro in that particular member state would end.

All these papers have one thing in common: Exit from the EMU would be very costly in political, economic, social, and market terms. The main economic cost is likely higher inflation and perhaps higher output variability as the economy readjusts to its local currency. Other legal aspects of rewriting agreements and contracts and reprogramming ATMs are large and could influence the initial adjustment phase materially. Regaining monetary and fiscal policy credibility will be tested by markets with the necessary volatility. At the December 2011 EU summit, further fiscal integration by introducing debt-brake legislation into constitutions was agreed to, and the European Commission would receive authority to approve or reject draft budgets before parliamentary submission. Yet the discussion among European politicians has intensified in relation to multiple orderly defaults, potential (voluntary) exits of countries, and deeper haircuts on government bonds. These were all fuel for a self-fulfilling prophecy. If politicians speak to exits and defaults, then markets will anticipate such. In the process, the bad outcome becomes reality.

The papers speak to an impossible exit or a very costly exit. But the exit is a product of the European political process that ultimately decides to make a change in the treaty that makes an exit legally possible. In the 1990s, Denmark, the United Kingdom, and Sweden approved the Maastricht Treaty but negotiated an opt-out clause of the euro, a clause that entails being part of the EU but not the EMU. This may be a historical precedent for how potentially an opt-out clause could be built into the treaty for several peripheral countries as the European politicians aim at unique and separate solutions. However, opting out also proved costly during that period in the 1990s: Not only did the ERM system implode as a "parallel" currency system, but the ECU did not have the credibility of the markets, and the United Kingdom, Denmark, and Sweden (banking crisis) all went through a significant contraction and financial system deleveraging.

The "Grexit"

In February 2012, economist Willem Buiter coined the term "Grexit,"referring to the possibility that Greece might exit the monetary union during the course of 2012 into 2013. By May 6, 2012, the Greek election outcome raised expectations that Greece was on the verge of such an exit. There were two kinds of domino effects at work. One was that the Greek exit would become a self-fulfilling outcome fueled by expectations and statements by officials that an exit by Greece was "technically manageable." Contingency plans were drafted that led to caution, which in turn led to capital and deposits withdrawal. Once such withdrawal was noticed, risk aversion increased, leading to more capital withdrawal from European sovereign bond markets. This further affected confidence and financial conditions in European economies. The other domino effect was a "standoff" between multiple players that caused further coordination problems. The fact that central bank officials, the head of the IMF, and European politicians spoke openly of the possibility of an exit by Greece caused officials from foreign central banks and other countries to suggest the same. What was first thought to be a theoretical probability became reality, a self-fulfilling prophecy. Such political statements were instantly transmitted through financial markets via flight to quality to liquid government bonds, higher volatility across markets, and a widening of risk premiums. The standoff took place on the streets of Europe, where growing protests against austerity brought along "social-political rejection." The street protests inspired radical left- or rightwing local politicians to run against the pro-austerity technocratic establishment.

Parties in other countries took notice, such as the True Finns in Finland, the Pirates Party in Germany, and the Party for People and Freedom in the Netherlands. The other standoff was a shift of political power in France, the Netherlands, and Greece, in opposition to Germany, which throughout the crisis had taken a dominant role in directing policy changes with respect to European fiscal governance rules. The combination of official statements related to an inevitable exit of a country from the monetary union, economic contraction, accelerated deposit and capital withdrawal, and social-political rejection made the Grexit a domino phenomenon that encompassed all three kinds of social-political, economic, and financial effects. Whichever way Greece would eventually exit, the possibility had increased that the monetary union would cease to exist in its current form, and in turn a Greek exit could be the first step for other countries to follow, in accordance with the domino theory.

Lessons: The Noise Factor

The Euro-zone debt crisis has many elements of the financial domino framework described in Chapter 1. It has sociopolitical factors that have had a major influence so far. The intensity of the crisis has been caused in part by political disagreements that fueled uncertainty. This is the *noise factor*. The number of headlines from EU officials and diplomats that daily came over newswires such as Reuters and Bloomberg often caused confusion among market participants. That confusion turned into uncertainty, which turned into skepticism and then risk aversion. Perhaps former Greek Prime Minister Papandreou expressed the political noise factor most vividly by stating the following in an open letter to the EU in July of 2011:

> "Crunch time" has arrived, and there is no room for indecisiveness and errors such as

- taking decisions that in the end prove "too little, too late" to convince the markets we are serious;
- making compromises that satisfy our internal political "red lines" that in the end substitute tactical politics for sound management of the crisis (although I do recognize the problems some governments have and the democratic demand for a greater say of Parliaments in trying to deal with this crisis);
- failing to use in-depth technical analysis and consultation before decisions are made;
- allowing a cacophony of voices and views to substitute for a shared agenda, thereby creating more panic than security.

As the number of summits increased, so did sovereign yields, and in reaction even more summits were held. The threat of public referendums and the trend of increasingly ultra right-wing or ultra left-wing parties in minority governments and coalitions can undermine the fiscal compact made at the European level. Even if there is agreement on deficit and debt rules, this isn't to say that these rules will be adhered to by national governments. Papandreou's letter in fact addresses Murphy's law: "Everything that can go possibly wrong will go wrong."

The European debt crisis is an economic domino, as the twin-deficits analysis has shown. The sovereign contagion affecting the banking system is the financial domino aspect. Combined, the Euro-zone debt crisis has all three major dominoes running until at some point they meet each other and collide. As analyzed in detail, a crisis such as the one in the Euro zone has set the precedent for potential other sovereign crises if the mix among liquidity, solvency, economy, and policy is not balanced. The domino style of effects had multiple layers and remained in place throughout. The kind of side effects the debt crisis had on other markets, policy makers' reactions, and economies have made the investment universe even more complex. The transition from the great moderation to the great deliberation of what the outcomes of the crisis could be brings about a battlefield between risk-averse and risk-appetite investors. That battlefield and the accompanying volatility prove difficult to navigate, which is what the concluding Chapter 8 will address.

Chapter 8

Conclusion: Strategies for Navigating Volatile Markets

Previous chapters have painted a complex picture. Financial domino effects are complex because they intertwine between different variables, players, economies, and social systems. Complexity is what investors are facing when they navigate financial markets in an age of austerity. Unlike the age of the "great moderation," where leverage drove risk premiums to the narrowest ever seen and volatility to the lowest ever witnessed, the financial crisis changed this not just by one cataclysmic event but by many domino effects that took place in the aftermath. The great moderation was perhaps known as an era ex-domino effects, an era of low, compressed volatility. Although not entirely as the VIX index (the Chicago Board Options Exchange Volatility Index that reflects a market estimate of the future volatility of the S&P 500 Index) shows in Figure 8.1, there were "bumps" along the way until the big bang spike in volatility in 2008. The frequency of volatility bumps has increased since 2008 as the European sovereign debt crisis, the European banking crisis, and the sluggish world economy created an all but certain environment where different scenarios and outcomes

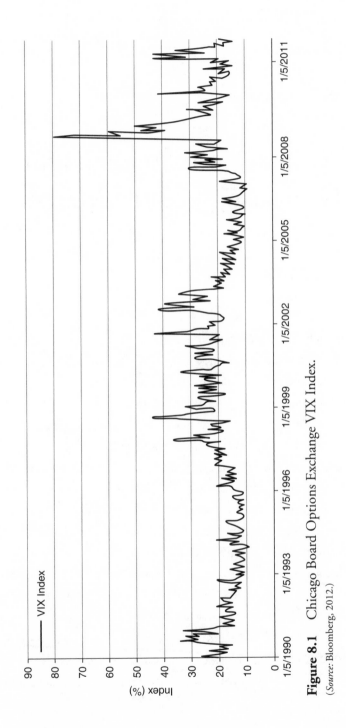

Figure 8.1 Chicago Board Options Exchange VIX Index.

(*Source:* Bloomberg, 2012.)

204

are possible. This is the age where domino effects can intensify and follow in greater numbers.

A strategy to navigate these uncharted waters in markets is one of dual construction—a "risk on and "risk off" portfolio. As the preceding chapters showed, symptoms, policy reactions, and contagion look to be here to stay until the global economy finds a more sustainable and structurally higher growth path. Reaching that path is going to be treacherous. The aging of populations and their motivation to save rather than spend, the multiple speeds of public- and private-sector deleveraging, and the duality in outcomes such as serial inflation and defaults all present headwinds. Knowing those headwinds, reaching the path to higher growth also requires a map, where it has to be said that by no means are the headwinds predictable. To start with, the diagram of the financial domino framework presented in Chapters 1 and 2 can provide a guide. For each main domino effect element of the diagram, there is a portfolio strategy to apply—one that can "protect" against a bad outcome (e.g., war, inflation, and default) and one that can "benefit" from a good outcome (e.g., large policy responses and an improved economic cycle). A portfolio could consist of multiple strategies that could be run in an all-in-one manner. There are risks, however. One is correlation between assets, and another is the appropriate weighting and, of course, the right timing in making investments.

Modern portfolio theory says that in order to have meaningful comparisons of returns across different portfolios, risk normalization analysis must be performed. And a distinct differentiation can be made between risk-averse investors, who strictly prefer a less risky portfolio for a given level of expected returns, and risk-appetite investors, who want outside benchmark positioning. To quantify risk-averse and risk-appetite investors, a widely used measure of risk-adjusted performance is the *Sharpe ratio*, alternatively known as the *information ratio*. This ratio simply states that investors should compare portfolios based on their expected excess returns per unit of volatility. This is consistent with investors' desire to minimize overall portfolio volatility subject to a desired level of expected returns, in other words, to equivalently maximize expected return for a given level of volatility. Such maximization of returns is optimal when the principle of "not putting all your eggs in one basket" is applied. The key is diversification among different types of assets to achieve a successful record of investing, along with making timely decisions. After 2008, another challenge presented itself as the normal distribution of asset returns became flatter and the tails became fatter. This is a direct effect of financial deleveraging stemming from asset liquidations as well as lower interest rates owing to zero-bound policies. This environment created the notion of *tail risks*. A tail risk is technically a risk of a portfolio value move of at least 3 standard deviations from the mean and tends to be more probable than what would be anticipated by a normal distribution. The appropriate tail hedge is widely debated, and the most applied are option strategies in currency, equities, and bonds. With any option, the time decay and understanding of what gives the option value, namely, volatility and expectations thereof, are key variables to the success of a tail hedge. In the end, the premium paid is an opportunity cost forfeiting expected return to guard against principal loss. Analogous to buying earthquake insurance, the premium paid has to be worthwhile when disaster strikes. In California, it has been warned for years that a large quake is well overdue. Thus each person needs insurance in case of a disaster. The rolling premium is an annual cost many people pay automatically, but they may forget whether it is the right insurance for them, whether it is competitively priced, and, most important, whether the insurance delivers what is expected during moments of greatest need. Even though the outcome of a large earthquake is viewed by each insurance company with approximately the same average probability, the insurance premiums vary greatly. The reason is that the risk itself varies as well; that is, there is risk that is diversifiable and risk that is systemic. An earthquake is an example of systemic risk. Within the concept of the financial domino framework, it can be argued that sociopolitical, economic, and financial dominoes all have systemic risk as well as nonsystemic risk elements.

Taking various degrees of risk as a starting point, constructing a portfolio based on the financial domino framework must take into account that there is a difference between asset and risk diversification. The importance here is that asset composition should be less risky than the individual assets themselves. This can be accomplished by diversification or hedging, which, in turn, relies on return correlations where a near-zero to mildly positive correlation is optimal diversification and negative correlation is optimal hedging. Diversification and hedging have an inherent *basis*—the cost-price difference between portfolio assets and hedge assets. This basis is a risk, a mismatch between what is perceived as attractive assets and what is perceived to be protection. Asset returns therefore reflect covariance that exists in a portfolio owing to the number of assets it holds. Given a broader investment opportunity set, returns generated from well-diversified portfolios ought to be superior to those provided by less diversified portfolios for a given level of risk. The benefits of diversification have been known and studied for over 60 years, with the basic idea that by combining different assets, an overall better risk and return profile can be achieved than by holding individual assets correlated among asset returns.

For example, measured from data provided by Bloomberg, from 1990 until the present, the annualized average return and volatility of the Barclays U.S. Aggregate Bond Index was approximately 7.1 percent and 3.9 percent, respectively, for a ratio of return to volatility of 1.84. Similarly, for the S&P 500 index, the average return and volatility were 10.2 and 15 percent, respectively, with a return-volatility ratio of 0.68. Provided that investors' preferences are to maximize the expected return-volatility ratio of their portfolios and that these expectations can be well approximated by long-term historical averages, then clearly U.S. fixed-income securities would be the natural investment choice. However, by investing a small portion in U.S. equities, for example, 95 percent in bonds and 5 percent in equities, it is possible to achieve an even better return-volatility ratio of 1.88. The higher the return-volatility ratio, the more excess return is given the level of volatility.

The factor of arbitrage then also becomes relevant when dealing in a higher-volatility environment. In this context, the *arbitrage pricing theory* (APT) is applicable. The APT, proposed by Stephen Ross in 1976, describes assets as mispriced when they diverge from the factor model. The arbitrageur selects "correctly" priced assets by weighting them so that the portfolio beta per factor is the same as for a portfolio that holds mispriced assets. Because it is long and short perfect and has mispriced assets, the portfolio has a positive expected return (difference between asset return and portfolio return), which implies that the total portfolio has a net zero exposure to macroeconomic volatility. The arbitrageur thus is in a position to make a "risk-free" profit when exchanging perfect and mispriced assets. The APT says that security returns are explained by factors such as surprises in inflation, growth but also sudden changes in default premiums, and shifts in the yield curve. This is unlike the other theory, the *capital asset pricing model* (CAPM), which says that a market portfolio determines a required rate of return given the level of undiversifiable risk.

In today's marketplace, which could be described as a risk-on and risk-off environment, the basics of the APT have some merit. For an analysis in relation to financial domino effects, four portfolios are considered. Portfolio A is that of a risk-averse investor, and the portfolio is positioned in longer government bonds, underweight in corporate bonds, and no or limited equity exposure. In addition excess cash is invested in Treasury bills. Portfolio B is that of a risk-appetite investor, with holdings invested in a combination of corporate bonds, equities, derivatives, and mortgage-backed securities. Cash is invested in asset-backed securities and floating-rate notes. Portfolios A and B represent the private sector and so combined can be viewed as risk-on (long) and risk-off (short) total portfolios. Portfolios A and B may have been the general description of private-sector portfolios in the past, but now that central banks are engaged in financial markets, one needs also to consider public-sector portfolios. A similar division can be made. Portfolio C is that of a central bank that holds a combination of government bonds, mortgages, and structured credit securities. Portfolio D is that of a central bank that solely holds government bonds across all maturities. If the APT theory holds, then portfolios A through D could have arbitrage within their constituents and relative to one another.

One must consider the economic scenarios and potential outcomes that reflect the positioning of portfolios A through D. In the case of the private sector, portfolio A would be chosen when investors expect a weak economy and are uncertain about the path ahead. Portfolio B reflects optimism, risk-taking, and high spirits, and would be chosen when expectations of higher economic growth materialize. In the case of the public sector, it is the other way around. Portfolio C would be chosen in times of market distress across all asset classes and when the economy worsens significantly. A central bank then would be seeking to deploy all kinds of quantitative and credit easing. Portfolio D is related to portfolio C but with solely government bond holdings, its composition is a reflection of the bank's expectations of a normal growth cycle. And then there are the outcomes, stipulated in Chapter 5 as the good and bad equilibria. Portfolios A and C would be suited for a bad equilibrium that sees flight to quality, steep yield curves, high volatility across asset classes, and creative, intense monetary policy actions. An outcome could be a series of defaults across companies and governments. Portfolios B and D could fare well in a good equilibrium. Where deleveraging and austerity end, there is a healthy level of inflation, and return expectations and monetary policy are more conventional. An extreme version would be where inflation runs well above a long-term average.

The distinction in scenarios and outcomes is influenced by socio-political, economic, and financial domino effects. The central banks play a crucial role in fighting those effects, as described in Chapter 4. Moreover, how a central bank goes about this is by playing arbitrageur within its own portfolio and with the private sector. The central bank is in a position to willingly engineer the yield curve, the risk premium, and default arbitrage. The portfolio balance effect is an example thereof and one to reckon with because that technique could be applied more often than not to generate risk-on environments to facilitate an orderly debt deleveraging process. There also could be switching between interest-rate risk and credit risk, influenced by central bank actions in an attempt to defuse solvency risk. And when the central bank temporarily creates a risk-on environment, risk premiums narrow on reduction of illiquidity as risk aversion recedes. When the effect fades and realization resurfaces that returns were inflated, risk aversion returns.

There is also the notion of how different asset classes compare with one another after the 2008 crisis. Figure 8.2 is taken from the Barclays research titled, "Equity Gilt Study." The figure shows that

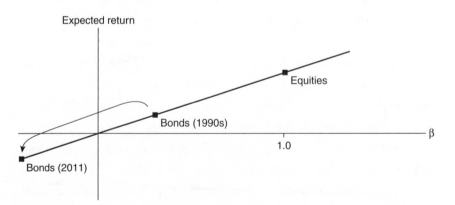

Figure 8.2   Bond versus equity risk premium.
(*Source:* Barclays Capital Research, "Equity Gilt Study 2012.")

government bonds today are excessively overvalued when measured against equities in terms of expected returns relative to their beta, the sensitivity of an individual stock against the market's entire sensitivity. If the APT were to hold, the beta-weighted portfolio of bonds and stocks would favor stocks. Barclays makes the case that the equity risk premium is now higher thanks to an acute scarcity of safe assets owing to continuous downgrades that have shrunk the AAA-rated government bond universe. Moreover, this is also the case because of forms of financial repression engendered by central banks that continue fighting liquidity traps by removing "safe" government bond assets from the private sector. As long as that is the case, the arbitrage between public and private sectors remains in place.

This has an important implication for portfolio allocation between fixed-income securities and equity. According to a study by Credit Suisse's *Global Investment Returns Yearbook 2011*, the return differences between U.S. equities and bonds have shifted markedly. From 1900 until the present, equities returned 6.3 percent in annualized real terms, whereas bonds returned just 1.8 percent. Narrowing the time frame from 1980 until today, the real return on bonds was about equal to that of stocks, approximately 6 percent. Over that time, U.S. real gross domestic product (GDP) growth, according to Bloomberg data, was approximately 2.6 percent. Thus returns on both stocks and bonds had an inherent flow of savings behind them.

This questions the appropriate weighting between stocks and bonds. Finance theory such as that by Modigliani and Miller, published in 1958, states that the change in the capital structure does not have any material effect on the value of the firm. Their main argument is that when either debt or equity changes, the weights of the two change proportionally and just enough that the change in the cost of debt would be offset by a change in the cost of equity. The reason is that debt typically has priority over equity, and the amount of debt financing changes the risk of equity. Modigliani and Miller do not account for the fact that when debt levels change, the risk of the cash flows of the company changes because there are indirect costs to debt, such as bankruptcy costs, legal costs, customers who walk away, and suppliers who do not deliver because the company is perceived as more risky.

Thus the weighting of bonds and stocks in a portfolio relies on the cost of each, whereas the cost of debt currently stands at record lows. As Figure 8.2 shows, bonds today have more negative beta sensitivity with stocks, making bonds a strong diversification tool even with yields at paltry levels. Credit Suisse's *Global Investment Returns Yearbook 2011* shows that bonds have a lower standard deviation, averaging around 12.5 percent across 19 major bond markets, whereas the global average for equities is around 23.4 percent. The correlation between bonds and stocks is low, and as the Credit Suisse research demonstrates, over a time frame from 1900 to 2010, there was a negative correlation between bond real returns and equity real returns. Measured for the major two markets, this correlation is –0.14 for the United States and –0.03 for the United Kingdom. Since stocks and bonds are at the outer ends of each equilibrium (good and bad), the negative correlation between them provides a source of return.

When constructing a portfolio, there are a few other factors to take into account. The first is the expected drawdown. The *drawdown* is defined as the difference between the portfolio's market value on a particular day and its maximum all-time-high market value. The interval from the date of the all-time-high market value to breaching that value is also called the *recovery period*. The investment is said to be *under water* from the date of the all-time-high mark to the end of the recovery period. The other factor is *tracking error*, the root mean square of the difference between the portfolio's return and that of its benchmark, a measure of how actively a portfolio is managed. A high tracking error describes the extent of outside index bets, and it attests to an active and risk-taking portfolio manager. Active management and frequent rebalancing of a portfolio may enhance the diversification, and a globally positioned portfolio would do so even more. Active management also entails higher transaction costs owing to frequent turnover. That said, liquid instruments such as futures contracts can minimize the cost.

In reality, there is no such thing as a perfect hedge or an optimal portfolio with a waterproof strategy that resembles a chicken that lays golden eggs continuously. And the financial domino effects described so far can severely affect what once looked like a well-balanced portfolio. There is also something called *basophobia*, the fear of falling down with an irrational view of gravitational pull. In investment terms, this fear is seen when investors buy securities that have already gained in value and may have peaked and see a drastic fall afterwards. The fact that investors bought Internet stocks near the peak of the Nasdaq in March 2000 is an example. Once the peak is reached, rationalization of value sets in against an unfavorable change in the economy, and this sets in motion a spiral of liquidations. The recent asset bubbles in stocks and housing have shown this. Whereas currently it is questioned whether commodities and bonds are in a bubble, these assets could experience a similar aftermath. The domino effects framework is a guide to how such bubbles could pop, not so much by prediction but rather by how each unique domino effect has a recurring sequence. In the following section, each major domino effect is revisited and discussed in the potentially appropriate portfolio context.

Sociopolitical Domino Strategy

A sociopolitical domino effect is hard to detect. The Middle East example showed how quickly such a crisis can spread via basic Internet communication. The outcome of such a crisis may be concluded easily, but a revolution, an uprising, or even a military coup is an unpredictable event. A strong theme underlying this is the *Minsky moment*, a phrase coined by Paul McCulley in 2008. The Minsky moment is a tipping point where the market switches from euphoria to decline, in other words, a moment when market sentiment swings from complacency to paranoia.

When this happens, the first thing that comes to mind is to buy hedges. Over long periods of time, whenever uncertainty becomes excessive, investors tended to flock to gold or cash. Either choice has an opportunity cost, one of foregone interest income and the other because of a premium that has to be paid. According Credit Suisse's *Global Investment Returns Yearbook 2011*, in the period from 1900 to 2011, gold gave a real return of 1.1 percent in sterling terms, and its value fluctuated widely. The benefit of holding gold is that its value in real terms is not reduced by inflation. Gold therefore may function as a safe haven for a risk-averse investor when the bad outcome is high inflation. Gold doesn't provide a stream of income like bonds do but does have storage value. Gold could be viewed as a safe haven when a sociopolitical domino effect causes a financial crisis that results in large-scale debt monetization. The path the Euro-zone debt crisis has followed thus far has been exactly like that, so gold has appreciated according to Bloomberg data, by 26 percent in annualized nominal terms and 22 percent in annualized real terms. These are historical returns and thus a gauge of how gold could behave in a crisis, but such a return is never guaranteed.

Another outcome of a sociopolitical domino effect could be a form of conflict or war situation. War premiums tend to be built into commodities because they are needed to manufacture weapons and transport fuel and food supplies for armies, among other things. Since 2003, when numerous Middle East, Iraq, and Afghanistan conflicts threatened the supply of oil, crude prices have risen in nominal and real terms by about 17 and 12.5 percent, respectively, according to Bloomberg data. Commodities such as crude experience demand when a sociopolitical domino results in war. The demand is insurance-driven rather than speculative-driven because buying commodity futures contracts, although relatively easy to trade, requires margin when settled. However, an excessive position in commodity contracts is not preferred in a portfolio because it also would likely increase correlation with other assets.

Higher energy prices tend to increase headline inflation. Instruments such as U.S. Treasury inflation-protected securities (TIPS) are designed to protect against the negative effects of higher inflation. The coupon interest received is fixed, but the notional principal of the bond is linked to inflation, as measured by the consumer price index (CPI). Thus, when the CPI rises on the month by one-tenth of a percent, the notional value of the TIPS goes up by that amount, with only a three-month accretion lag. In the process, the investor accrues interest based on an increased inflation adjusted principal. In the case of deflation, the principal adjusts for deflation and pays interest on the below-par inflation adjusted principal. This is also known as the *deflation floor*. The floor "guarantees" the holder of TIPS the greater of the inflation-adjusted principal or par value at maturity, whichever is higher. The volatility of TIPS has been known to be lower than that on nominal Treasury bonds because of the risk-premium component difference. The nominal bond yield could be viewed as a real yield (yield adjusted for inflation), an inflation expectation, and the uncertainty of inflation expectations. The yield on TIPS is called *real yield*, the yield based on the present value that is adjusted for inflation. TIPS real yields since their 1997 introduction have had a negative correlation of about −0.04 with U.S. Treasuries and −0.15 with the broader stock index, measured by Bloomberg data regression from 1997 until present. TIPS therefore offer qualities in an uncertain situation but also carry interest-rate risk like any other fixed-income security.

Cash is another hedge when extreme stress occurs. Cash has a storage cost that is higher than that of other instruments. For one, holding large sums of cash requires security either in a deposit box at a bank or at a residence. The security is the insurance cost paid for holding cash. Holding cash is not risk-free because it can be destroyed, lost, or stolen, and it could experience a fall in real value when inflation is high. The fee paid for holding a deposit is a tradeoff people are at times willing to make for holding cash, but even so, holding onto cash without having it invested is the loss of the opportunity for interest income. However, each portfolio should hold a small portion in cash—it is the most direct and liquid means when urgent margin calls or payments have to be met.

Putting cash in T-bills is an alternative to holding cash. There is a convenience yield in investing in T-bills, even if that yield can be negative (in nominal and real terms) at times of great distress. Above all, buying T-bills at government auctions at no fee while holding the securities at the U.S. Treasury (the safest warehouse that has less likelihood to be robbed or default) is an ideal stress strategy. Therefore, paying a low or even negative nominal rate on a Treasury bill or deposit is in this context a convenience. At the same time, T-bills continue to be in demand because investors are willing to accept a negative nominal return on a risk-free asset because holding it is cheaper than storing cash. Having said that, T-bills carry credit risk due to the possibility of default, whereas cash does not have credit risk.

In unpredictable outcomes, there is a saying that goes, "There are no atheists in foxholes." That is, a safeguard against an outcome that is hard and tangible is something that returns principal. A combination of cash, TIPS, gold, Treasury bills, and selective commodities may be desirable hedges in a general portfolio consisting of stocks and bonds, given that these instruments do carry interest-rate, liquidity, default, and volatility risk unlike cash.

Economic Domino Strategy

An economic domino mostly prevails through a multiplier effect that can be induced by the private as well as the public sector. From the three main domino effects, the economic version is probably the easiest to identify and predict. Prediction can be achieved with regression models to forecast growth, inflation, and employment. Identification, however, is made by carefully monitoring fiscal and monetary policy announcements as well as how the private sector and financial markets react to such announcements. *Fed watching*, or central bank analysis, is a key component of the economic domino strategy. A multiplier effect means acceleration in economic growth or downturn. Equities tend to return positively as growth momentum picks up but are poor in a downturn. For bonds, this is in principle the opposite. Hence the right blend of stocks and bonds plays a role here, but it can be different in weight in terms of time-varying weights.

Equity investing requires a bottom-up approach and intelligent stock picking. Stock valuation is a function of interest rates, economic variables, and company-specific factors. The economic domino effect ties directly into stocks even more so than bonds because bonds tend to respond more on expectations of central bank action than on the economy itself, unless there is a burst of inflation. Economic dominoes, once set in motion, have a more simplified outcome—either economic growth or recession. The aftermath of growth and recession is inflation and default, each a bad outcome. As argued earlier, higher inflation or inflation expectations would point toward an allocation to TIPS or inflation-sensitive assets in a portfolio. On the other hand, equities can work in an inflation environment as well. The Credit Suisse *Global Investment Returns Yearbook 2011* estimates that equities returned 5 to 6 percent in real terms during higher inflation times, beating bond returns by a wide margin.

When the outcome is default, bond selection becomes a bottom-up proposition. As argued in Chapter 5, a shift occurs from interest-rate risk to credit risk when the perception of liquidity and solvency narrows, something that has happened during the European debt crisis. The rapid shift in sentiment by investors, leading to sudden liquidations, changed the perception of how safe government bonds actually were. Since the coupon on a bond is tied to the solvency of the issuer, if the probability of default is perceived to be higher, a self-reinforcing spiral can happen where yields rise, which increases the default probability, and these probabilities themselves affect the yield. For the government bond universe in major developed markets, this has become the number one "threat" to expected return of the investment.

The expected return for a government bond typically consists of the sum of the yield plus components such as *carry* (the difference between coupon interest and the presumable rate of funding), *roll down* (the difference in yield when the bond ages in a year's time), *convexity* (the change in the bonds' price sensitivity to a change in interest rates), and *curve shift* (the gain or loss from changes in the slope of the yield curve). Another way to express the yield is as the sum of such risk premiums as liquidity, credit, inflation, term, and volatility. Premium compensates investors for the uncertainty of holding-period returns owing to changes in interest rates, actual versus expected inflation, and liquidity preferences. The expected return has further become a combination of supply and demand for government bonds that during tranquility experience elevation when credit risk is perceived to be nonexistent, the cost of borrowing is low, and demand is stable. When a change in demand happens, such as during the European debt crisis, and credit risk has reached a boundary, long-term debt sustainability is questioned, and investors' time horizons shift. As a result, prices on stable government bonds collapse, like what normally can be expected from high-yield corporate bonds. Figure 8.3 briefly revisits the multiple-equilibria idea, where point *A*, the point of stability, shifts to point *B*, the point of vulnerability, and subsequently shifts to point *C*, the point of distress. With government debt at record highs, as issuance trends showed in Chapter 5, every major government bond market is at risk of abstract multiple equilibria. Even as central banks

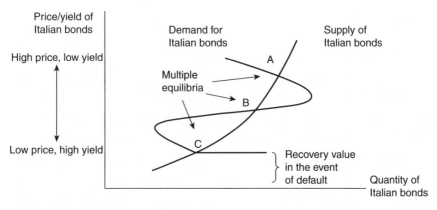

Figure 8.3   Multiple equilibria revisited.

keep their interest rates near zero, projected global economic growth remains low, and, with large outstanding government debt, increases the risk that more government bond markets will fall victim to multiple equilibria.

When an economic domino effect gets under way and growth expectations are adjusted downward, the nominal yield on bonds can fall or rise rapidly, depending on expected supply for given demand. To select the "best" kind of government bond, there are then a few basic selection criteria: (1) Does the central bank actively engage in the government bond market? (2) Is there is a captive domestic audience for the bonds? and (3) Are the bonds denominated in a domestic currency that can be freely printed? Currently, the only three bond markets that subscribe to all three criteria are U.S. Treasuries, U.K. gilts, and Japanese government bonds. For these three markets to experience significant distress, hyperinflation would have to occur, which at elevated debt levels may keep their central banks at near-zero rates. Thus, in an economic domino effect scenario, portfolio allocation to either of these government bond markets may be desirable, bearing in mind that government bonds are *not* free of sovereign default risk.

Financial Domino Strategy

Financial crises may recur more frequently than sovereign or economic crises because one of the main causes is leverage. Without leverage, financial crises would practically be nonexistent because the compounding effect of positions unwinding is what drives margin calls, funding disruptions, and liquidity distortions. Flight to liquidity, to quality, and to safety happens often, and to a degree, such capital flow coincides with what can happen during sociopolitical and economic domino effects. The difference with a financial crisis is that demand for certain assets is driven by collateral.

The other difference is correlation, when all risk assets trade with a correlation to 1, they trade like a one-way bet. The unwinding of risk assets then is equally correlated once confidence breaks and the market turns down. Once again, government bonds are the instrument to be positioned in because their liquidity premium is superior during such times and is also driven by collateral calls on demand. Other assets that tend to have unlevered beta include T-bills, cash, or alternatives to credit or securitized products, which lower the volatility of bonds issued by government agencies. Another effect of financial dominoes is volatility. Although volatility also increases for sociopolitical as well as economic reasons, financial crises have shown spikes in volatility owing to crowded option and financial futures contracts positioning.

Final Words

The Dutch were the first financial engineers of a tradable futures market. The futures contracts were based on a good exchange for tulips, a fad among wealthy Dutch merchants during Holland's "Golden Age" in the sixteenth century. The tulip was not native to Holland but rather was introduced in 1593 by a botanist named Carolus Clusius, who intended to do research on the plant for his medical practice. Another explanation suggests that tulips were imported from Turkey and contracted a virus, called a *mosaic virus*. This virus was not deadly to the flower but produced flames of color near the bottom of the pedal of the plant. This made the tulips even more exotic and appealing. Prices of the tulips rose sharply, and tulip traders made fortunes. Much like a domino effect, this caused a trading frenzy. Then, around 1636–1637, one of the main trading centers in Haarlem (a city near Amsterdam) experienced its first default on a payment by a single customer. An ensuing panic broke out, and the first financial bubble in history imploded in a rare product such as tulips circa 1637.

The importance of the tulip episode was not so much irrational behavior that led to its collapse, but rather how a futures market was changed by decree of the Dutch government as bulb prices soared through *windhandel*, a Dutch term for market speculation. The government's decree indicated that if bulb prices were to fall, there would be an option for the futures contract holder to pay a penalty (3.5 percent) and forgo the obligation to deliver bulbs. Thus the government changed the futures contract into an option contract, which resulted in an immediate halt of *windhandel* and led to the collapse of tulip prices. This example shows how an official sector that induces a change of agreements may entail a tradeoff: The investor can accept a penalty or face a capital loss.

In today's markets, investors have to face the same tradeoff. A portfolio bearing handsome index returns with the help of central bank or government intervention has to face risk at some point. This risk represents a dotted line between greed and fear. The balance between greed and fear is driven by hesitation, which in combination with fear causes further hesitation. Since hesitation could make the worst fears come true, navigating in artificially supported markets often challenges one as to when to hesitate and when not to hesitate. Recognizing that markets are fraught with *windhandel*, the financial domino framework

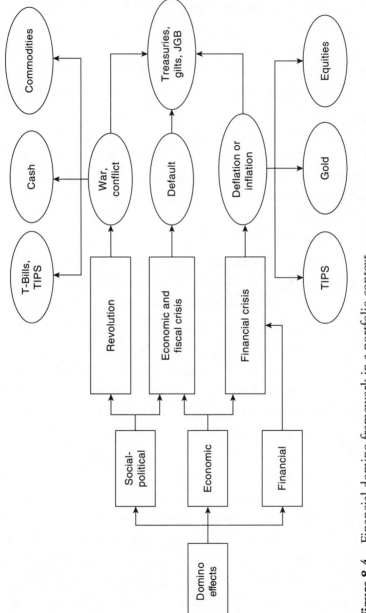

Figure 8.4 Financial domino framework in a portfolio context.

may provide a guide. Each of the domino effects strategies subscribes to a safety measure, an automatic hand break in a portfolio when it gets slippery. Figure 8.4 shows the framework once more with safety nets spun around the domino effects. The strategies are basic, and such basics are needed when a situation turns complex. Thus, having a portfolio with consistent risk-off components in cash, Treasury bonds, T-bills, gold, commodities, and TIPS and risk-on bottom-up equity selection of growth and dividend stocks may be an appropriate blend to achieve stable returns given that this kind of portfolio is not a guarantee to achieve such returns, taking into account that history doesn't always predict the future. With a domino effect stemming from ubiquity, flight to quality, a self-fulfilling prophecy, or even a systemic crisis, the strategy is based on protection against uncertainty. The uncertainty can remain in economies caught by liquidity traps, sovereign insolvency, inflation volatility, and political instability. Since nothing else is certain other than death and taxes, the domino framework provides investors with insight into how to navigate an uncertain world.

References

Chapter 1

Buchanan, Mark. *Ubiquity*. New York: Crown Publishers, 2001.

Eisenhower, Dwight D. Presidential press conference, April 7, 1954.

Merton, Frank K. *Social Theory and Social Structure*. New York: Free Press, 1968.

Tolstoy, Leo. *War and Peace* (1828). Reprint. New York: Vintage Classics.

Chapter 2

Bernanke, Ben. "Semiannual Monetary Policy Report." Federal Reserve, March 1, 2011.

Bernanke, Ben; Gertler, Mark; and Gilchrist, Simon. "The Financial Accelerator and the Flight to Quality," *Review of Economics and Statistics* 78(1), pp. 1–15, 1996.

"The Domino Effect." *The Economist*. July 3, 2008.

"Domino Theory: Assessing the Risk Greece Heralds Something Far Worse." February 18, 2010.

"France Goes Soft-Core." *The Economist*. January 14, 2012.

Fitch statement on European sovereign downgrades, December 16, 2011.

Keynes, John Maynard. *The General Theory of Employment Interest and Money* (1936). Reprint. New York: Classic Books America, 2009.

Standard & Poors statement on United States downgrade, August 6, 2011.

Standard & Poors statement on European sovereign downgrades, December 16, 2011.

Chapter 3

Gladwell, Malcolm. *The Tipping Point*. Boston: Little, Brown, 2002.

Li, David. "On Default Correlation: A Copula Function Approach." *Journal of Fixed Income* 9 (4), pp. 43–54, March 2000.

Lorenz, Edward. *The Essence of Chaos*. Seattle: University of Washington Press, 1995.

Masson, Paul. "Contagion: Monsoonal Effects, Spillovers, and Jumps Between Multiple Equilibria." IMF Working Paper No. 98/142.

Mink, Mark; and Haan, Jacob de. "Contagion During the Greek Sovereign Debt Crisis." DNB Working Paper No. 335, 2012.

Singh, Manmohan. "Velocity of Pledged Collateral." IMF Working Paper No. 11/256, 2011.

Standard & Poors. "Default Correlations; Empirical Evidence." 2002.

Chapter 4

Barro, Robert J.; and Gordon, David B. "Rules, Discretion, and Reputation in a Model of Monetary Policy." *Journal of Monetary Economics* 12, pp. 101–121, 1983.

Bernanke, Ben. "The Crisis and the Policy Response." At the Stamp Lecture, London School of Economics, London, U.K., 2009.

Chung, Hess; and LaForte, Jean-Philippe. "Estimating the Macroeconomic Effects of the Fed's Asset Purchases." San Francisco Federal Reserve, 2011.

D'Amico, Stepania; and King, Thomas. "Flow and Stock Effects of Large-Scale Treasury Purchases." New York Federal Reserve, 2010.

Dooley, Michael P.; Folkerts-Landau, David; and Garber, Peter. "An Essay on Revived Bretton Woods." National Bureau of Economic Research, Working Paper No. 9971, 2003.

Glic, Reuven; and Leduc, Sylvain. "Central Bank Announcements of Asset Purchases and the Impact on Global Financial and Commodity Markets." New York Federal Reserve, 2011.

Hicks, J. R. "Mr. Keynes and the Classics—A Suggested Interpretation." *Econometrica* 5, pp. 147–159, April 1937.

Lasaosa, Ana; Stevens, Ibrahim; and Tong, Matthew. "The Financial Market Impact of Quantitative Easing." Bank of England, 2010.

_____. The United Kingdom's Quantitative Easing Policy." Bank of England, 2010.

Minsky, Hyman. "The Financial Instability Hypothesis." *Handbook of Radical Political Economy.* Working Paper No. 74.

Neely, Christopher. "The Effects of Large-Scale Asset Purchases on TIPS Inflation Expectations." New York Federal Reserve, 2010.

_____. "The Large-Scale Asset Purchases Had Large International Effects." New York Federal Reserve, 2010.

Sack, Brian. "Large-Scale Asset Purchases by the Federal Reserve: Did They Work?" New York Federal Reserve, 2010.

Tobin, James. "Liquidity Preference as Behavior Towards Risk." *The Review of Economic Studies* 67, 1958.

Chapter 5

Amato, Jeffery. "The Role of the Natural Interest Rate in Monetary Policy." BIS Working Paper 171, 2005.

Bernanke, Ben. "Deflation: Making Sure "It" Doesn't Happen Here." Speech before the National Economists Club, Washington, D.C., 2002.

——. "The Global Savings Glut and the U.S. Current Account Deficit," 2005.

Grauwe, Paul de. "The Fragility of European Governance." CEPS Policy Brief, 2011.

Haldane, Andrew G. "The Short Long." 29th Société Universitaire Européene de Recherches Financières Colloquium: New Paradigms in Money and Finance." Brussels, 2011.

Hicks, John. "The Yield on Consuls." Paper read to the UK Manchester Statistical Society, 1958.

Koo, Richard. *The Holy Grail of Macroeconomics: Lessons from Japan's Great Recession.* John Wiley & Sons (Asia) Pte. Ltd., 2008.

Krugman, Paul. "Gross Confusion." *New York Times*, December 20, 2011.

——. "Japan's Trap," May 1998. Accessible from Krugman's website: www.wws.princeton.edu/~pkrugman.

"Monthly Forecast and Analysis of U.S. Economy and Financial Markets." *Bank Credit Analyst* 64/4, October 2011.

Reinhart, Carmen; and Rogoff, Kenneth. *This Time Is Different.* Princeton, NJ: Princeton University Press, 2010.

Say, Jean Baptiste. *Traite d'économique politique ou simple exposition de la manière dont se forment, se distribuent et se composent les richesses,* 1803. Translated from the fourth French edition as *A Treatise on Political Economy, or the Production, Distribution, and Consumption of Wealth.* Kitchener, Ontario: Batoche Books, 2001.

Smith, Adam. *Wealth of Nations* (1776).

Tett, Gillian. "Get Used to a World Without the 'Risk-Free' Rate." *Financial Times*, September 10, 2011.

Turner, Phillip. "Is the Long-Term Interest Rate a Policy Victim, a Policy Variable, or a Policy Lodestar?" Bank of International Settlements Working Paper No. 367, December 2011.

Walras, Léon. *Elements of Pure Economics* (1874–1877). Reprint. Routledge Library Editions, 2010.

Wicksell, Knutt. "The Influence of Interest and Price." *Economic Journal* 17, pp. 213–220, 1907.

Chapter 6

Dickens, William T. "How Wages Change: Micro Evidence from the International Wage Flexibility Project." European Central Bank Working Paper No. 697, November 2006.

Grauwe, Paul de. *The Economics of Monetary Union.* 7th ed. Oxford: Oxford University Press, 2007.

Krugman, Paul. *New York Times* blogs. "The Conscience of a Liberal: Austria," April 15, 2009.

Mundell, Robert A. "A Theory of Optimum Currency Areas." *American Economic Review* 51/4, pp. 657–665, September 1961.

Chapter 7

Athanassiou, Phoebus. "Withdrawal and Expulsion from the EU and EMU." ECB Legal Working Paper No. 10, December 2009.

EFSF. Legal documents: available at http://www.efsf.europa.eu/about/legal-documents /index.htm.

Eichengreen, Barry. "The Breakup of the Euro Area." NBER Working Paper No. 13393, September 2007.

EU statement, July 21, 2011.

EU statement, October 26, 2011.

EU statement, December 9, 2011.

EU statement, February 20, 2012.

"Firefighting: The Sovereign-Debt Crisis Has Echoes of the ERM Debacle." *The Economist.* July 14, 2011.

"Greece: Preliminary Debt Sustainability Analysis." IMF, 2012.

Papandreou, George. Open letter to the European Union, July 11, 2011. Available at http://www.asymptotix.eu/printpdf/news/Papandreou-open-letter-president-euro group-jean-claude-juncker.

Sargent, Thomas J.; and Wallace, Neil. "Some Unpleasnt Monetarist Arithmetic." Federal Reserve Bank of Minneapolis, 1981.

Sokos, Ioannis. "Greek PSI: Questions and Answers." BNP Paribas Research, 2012.

Chapter 8

Kantor, Larry. "Equity Gilt Study." Barclays Research, 2012.

Modigliani, F.; and Miller, M. "The Cost of Capital, Corporation Finance, and the Theory of Investment." *American Economic Review* 48(3): 261–297, 1958.

O'Sullivan, Michael; and Kersley, Richard. *Credit Suisse Global Investment Returns Yearbook 2011.* Credit Suisse Research Institute, 2011.

Index

About the Author

Ben Emons is a senior vice president and portfolio manager in the global portfolio management group at Pacific Investment Management Company (PIMCO), in Newport Beach, California. Prior to joining PIMCO in 2008, he was a portfolio manager at Nuveen Investments in Los Angeles, focusing on government bonds and derivatives. Prior to his experience in the United States, he worked for ABN AMRO Bank N.V. in derivatives trading and fixed income strategy and research. He has 16 years of investment experience and holds an MBA from the University of Southern California's Marshall School of Business and a master's degree in international finance from the University of Amsterdam, the Netherlands. Mr. Emons is a frequent contributor to PIMCO's *Global Central Bank Focus*, writes a monthly column for the Dutch financial newspaper *Het Financieele Dagblad*, and has written about a range of other topics on PIMCO's website (www.pimco.com).